YOUR TIME WILL COME

JACK YERMAN
AND HIS INCREDIBLE JOURNEY TO THE
1960 OLYMPICS

Bruce Hamilton Yerman

Paperback ISBN: 978-0-557-19765-1

Hardcover ISBN: 978-1-300-51490-9

All photographs courtesy of Jack and Margo Yerman

To Sarah, Bryce, Blake, and Brook,
and the champions who follow.

Jack Yerman

World Records
Mile Relay
1600-Meter Relay
Two-Mile Relay
Distance Medley Relay
European Sprint Medley Relay
Indoor 400-Meter Short Track
660-Yard Sprint (Unofficial)

U.S. National Championships
Indoor 600 Meters (Twice)
Outdoor 400 Meters
Olympic Trial 400 Meters
Mile Relay

Major Events
First US-USSR Dual Meet, 1958
Rose Bowl, 1959
Olympic Gold Medal, 1600-Meter Relay, 1960
Pan American Games
Council International Military (CISM),
International Champion, 1961-1963
Germany-United States Indoor Meet, Berlin, 1965

Honors
All-American, Track and Field
All University of California Athlete, Junior Year
University of California, Hall of Fame
Sacramento Area Sports Hall of Fame
Woodland Sports Hall of Fame
Outstanding Service—
Paradise High School Athletic Hall of Fame

I grew up listening to my father's stories. He shared his memories in quiet places, such as driving to a basketball game or when working together in the yard or holding our weekly family meetings. Once in a while, I accompanied him when he spoke to groups of young people. These stories are told the way I heard them. Several chapters begin with a childhood experience that Jack connects to something learned on his road to the Olympics.

PROLOGUE

Is It True?

Hanna sat in front of her computer, her finger twisting through a brown curl that had escaped down her forehead. She sat remembering the U.S. History teacher she had met two years earlier, third period on the first day of school. She had watched him while he watched students crisscross the room to find a seat. She had noticed his bright blue eyes from behind the timeless horn rimmed glasses that sat comfortably on his bald head, with a touch of gray hair above his ears. She wondered how long ago the friendly worry lines had become permanent across his forehead, and she liked his gentle smile peeking through a casual, almost scruffy, beard.

Hanna took her seat on the first row directly facing the teacher's desk. The face of the desk was painted with a red, white, and blue Superman exploding towards her, his fist pushing upward, the other tucked aerodynamically by his side. The superhero bore the teacher's glasses on the same round head. The numerous nicks and scratches on the work of art told Hanna that the student who had produced it had long since moved on.

Hanna remembered how Chico's warm summer days had blended into a mild California autumn. She had watched the leaves of the giant twisted oak outside the classroom yellow, dry, and fall away. Hanna was sixteen at the time, an exchange student from the Netherlands at Chico High School. Her English improved with each passing week. History was her favorite class. She anticipated each day's revelations. She sat captivated along with the other students listening to the teacher's stories as if he had been there breathing, smelling, seeing and touching what others only read about in books.

It had been two years since Hanna had returned to her home country. She sat pondering, "How could his stories be true?" How could this bulky, balding, bespectacled teacher be the younger, slimmer, taller witness of the history he shared? She had imagined someone more attractive in his stories. Had she fallen for the teacher's deception, a trick of a master performer who made her believe in things that were not quite true—like the Superman painted on his desk?

Determined to put her frustration behind, Hannah leaned towards her computer, opened her E-mail and pounded a letter onto the monitor:

Date:	Friday, October 2, 1998
From:	Hanna
Subject:	Are your stories true?

I was an exchange student in your American History class. I don't know if you remember me, but anyway, I have a question that often pops into my mind: Are your stories true? You covered a lot of history, and it has bothered me because the information you gave cannot be found anywhere. It would mean a lot if I knew whether a "Jack-story" was made up to make me pay attention; or, were you actually part of all these things?

Hanna rested her hands on the keyboard for a moment before hitting *Send.* If the teacher had been honest with her, if his stories had been true, if he had been part of history, perhaps she too could be a force in her world as he had been in his. She read her E-mail again because if it were not true, it would all be forgotten.

Hanna wrinkled the fading freckles on her nose and hit *Send.*

Contents

CHAPTER 1

Wanting It

The more I coached the more I became convinced that the mind, the will, the determination, the mental approach to competition are of the utmost importance. Yes, perhaps even more than the improvements in form and technique.

All of us have seen men of average ability—who strive to be something other than average—succeed in athletics.

We have seen it in other walks of life as well. We coaches don't understand it as yet. Nor am I certain that psychologists do. But this motivating power of the mind is a force we all reckon with and a force that all coaches, directly or indirectly, try to direct.

Coach Brutus Hamilton
(Walton, 1992)

When asked how long he trained for the Olympics, Jack will typically answer, "Three or four years." Many who ask are looking for a quick answer—a two-and-a-half minute success story. Several years after the Olympics, Jack asked Mr. Bailey, his former high school basketball coach, why, of all his teammates, he ran faster, traveled the world, played in the Rose Bowl, and graduated from the University of California and Stanford when others who had more talent did not. The coach replied, "It was important to you. You wanted it more than the others."

"I wanted it?"

Jack remembered his junior year in high school when he sat daydreaming in class and doodling on his physics paper. He wrote in the upper corner, "Gold Medal, 1960 Olympics. 400 meters." Sitting behind him was Cummings, a cocky boy who peaked over Jack's shoulder.

"You're stupid!" he derided. "You'll never do that." Up to that point, Jack had never won a race, but something inside said, *Your time will come.*

Jack's childhood home, 122 Fourth Street
Woodland, California

Wanting it began in his childhood home on 122 Fourth Street, in Woodland, California. Jack was a year old in 1940. The average home value in California was $3,527 dollars (U.S. Census Bureau), and Mom and Gram had pooled their resources to purchase a small, one bedroom home for $500. It once had been a chicken coop on a long-ago farm, and it took Irene ten years to pay off the mortgage. Mom slept in the twin bed during the day, and the boy, Jack, shared it with his sister at night, their heads pointing in opposite directions.

Jack never heard the words *I love you* in his home. He did not know that other mothers cradled their children and read to them before bed. The sanctuary of a loving hand pulling blankets up around his ears and feeling a mother's gentle kiss on the forehead was unknown to Jack. Words trickled from her mouth like sparse gravel. She never attended a church social, she never chatted with other women about the rising cost of milk, and she never gossiped about a neighbor. She never made a friend.

Irene was a thin woman. Her graying black hair was always short, requiring little attention. Her work wardrobe boasted a pair of white nurse's uniforms, and she walked silently in her soft white hospital shoes. At home, she threw on a housedress patterned with tiny flowers that had long since faded from repeated hand washing in the galvanized steel tub.

Irene sat for hours at the kitchen table, her sad blue eyes framed behind cat-eye glasses that curved upward to a point, staring at an imaginary spot somewhere on the bare white wall, her lips pursed around a cigarette and her left fingers forever tainted from the two packs a day while her right hand wrapped around a cup of day-old, bitter black coffee. Her mouth was in constant motion with or without the cigarette. Her furrowed lips puckered up and down, moving in and out, muscles randomly chewing like a cow on its cud.

Irene's timeless routine continued. The same yellow taxi transported her to Woodland Hospital five days a week, year after year. She earned an extra ten cents an hour working nights to support her two children and her mother, Bessie Flame, known as Gram. Whenever possible, Irene volunteered for extra shifts. The yellow taxi deposited her back home, smelling of the tobacco she smoked and the sick people she tended.

Irene Yerman
Nursing School Graduate

Irene seldom spoke. When she did, her slow and deliberate speech communicated basic everyday essentials. "We need to pay the electric bill." "I'm working an extra shift tonight." "Jack needs a new shirt. His other is ripped."

Jack's world of few words collided with first grade. In September of 1944, he entered school. He watched the other children say *RED* when the teacher held up the flash card of a fire truck. They all said *YELLOW* looking at the flash card with a happy sun. They all said *BLUE* when she pointed to the pond with the duck floating in the middle. Some of his classmates saw the *A* in *APPLE* and the *B* in *BOY* and the *Z* in *ZEBRA*, but Jack had never been exposed to the alphabet or basic school words in his home.

When others did not help Jack, he heard a still, small, comforting voice that seemed to whisper in his ear. It was a warm and kind voice, a man's voice, which reassured him when things did not go well. This unseen comforting companion filled his mother's emotionally absent gaps, softly speaking, *"Don't worry, your time will come."*

Jack and his sister, Kathy

Irene was reared a Baptist but did not claim any religion. She accompanied Jack and Kathy to the Methodist church on Christmas and Easter Sunday because it was only a few blocks from home. On those special days, she sat next to Jack until the compelling need for nicotine forced her away from the sermon. The remaining Sundays, through the four seasons, Mom and Kathy, Jack's older sister by two years, remained home while he dressed himself in his cleanest clothes, pushed his blond curly hair into order, and ran four blocks to the church. The congregation welcomed the boy who came alone and recited the Bible stories, sang the songs, and helped the minister and Sunday school teachers for five years without missing a Sunday. Jack puffed out his chest to receive his achievement bars that were pinned to his perfect attendance medals.

Sitting at home, Irene read her Bible, underlining passages with a pencil—she marked Proverbs more than the other books.

A good name is to be chosen rather than great riches,
and loving favour rather than silver or gold (Proverbs 22:1).

Withdraw thy foot from thy neighbor's house;
lest he be weary of thee, and so hate thee (Proverbs 25:17).

When Jack was born on February 5, 1939, his father, Loyd with one L, sat behind the bars of the Butte County Jail—the family guesses it was a fight, or maybe he was drunk, or maybe he owed someone money, or maybe it was everything. The hospital clerk in Oroville wrote "Common Laborer" on the birth certificate. Jack's father had been a sunbaked broncobuster who wandered from one Northern California ranch to another. Loyd was good with ropes. He was fast on a horse and could lasso with the best, circling the noose overhead and finding the stretched out neck of a terrified colt or the hind legs of a bawling calf on a dead run. Gritty work, wicked four-legged beasts, lonely bruises, and broken bones found solace in his growing consumption of painkillers and cheap alcohol.

Irene divorced the man before the boy's first birthday. She said only that it was best for the children, and years later she told Jack that his father had a hankering for prostitutes. In time, Jack learned that Loyd had molested Kathy when she was a small child. After years of living in a stupor of drugs and alcohol on the streets of Old Sacramento, Loyd walked into the County Hospital and died of a heart attack on the waiting room floor at the age of fifty-five.

Bronco Bustin' Loyd Yerman

Gram fed and watered the children while Irene slept during the day. Gram was a cookie-jar-shaped woman with a bulbous nose caught between her blue eyes. She rolled up her long hair in a conventional bun on the back of her head and never wore anything fancier than a simple cotton housedress. She caught rain water in a barrel for washing. She cooked pancakes for breakfast and made peanut butter sandwiches for lunch. Dinner varied between cheap pork chops or liver and onions with canned vegetables and potatoes. At month's end, when money was in short supply, the children ate milk and toast that Gram warmed on the stove. The children never had snacks. They roamed the neighborhood after meals, and the extent of Gram's discipline for the boy was simply to say to Irene, "You need to speak to your son."

At each summer's end, Jack's lopsided and torn black leather Oxfords could barely contain his growing feet, and his scuffed knees peaked through the lingering white threads of his fading jeans. While his mother slept, Gram walked Jack to town for a new pair of shoes and one new pair of dark blue shrink-to-fit Levi's and an expensive Pendleton shirt; his only new clothes for the year. J.C. Penney had a layaway plan where a little money down reserved the jeans and the shirt until Gram could pay in full. The Sacramento Valley's heavy heat beat down hard in August while Penney's ventilating swamp coolers pushed a refreshing breeze through the store. Gram pulled Jack past the colorful displays of pearly-button shirts that seemed to wave at him in the gentle flow of cool air. They walked past the stacks of blue, gray, black, and brown pants. If Jack asked Gram for anything beyond the shopping assignment, she would later tell Irene to talk to the boy. "Clothes don't make the man," Irene would say; but the quiet, small, comforting voice would interrupt Jack's disappointment, and he would hear, *"Your time will come."*

Jack inhaled the pleasing aroma of processed cotton while he and Gram waited for the clerk. Gram explained to the man that the boy needed new pants. The man pulled out his white tape and measured the boy's bony waist. "Twenty-six inches," said the man, so that is what Gram bought. He pulled the chosen size of pocket-riveted jeans, holding them up to Jack—Jack knew that they would be too small but would stretch as they did last year. Gram paid the clerk twenty-five cents to hold the pants on a special shelf until she could come up with the full two dollars and fifty cents.

The people of Woodland bought shoes at Emil's on Main Street. A middle-aged salesman with a wide smile and a gold tooth welcomed his customers and talked of the warm day. He sat Jack down and moved the sliders on the metal measuring device to the boy's toes and instep. "You know," the man said, "people spend three-fourths of the day in their shoes so it's gotta be properly fitted for a boy like this to grow strong." The man disappeared for a moment before returning with the selected shoe. Jack slid his foot inside, and the man cinched the laces. Jack stood and walked across the floor to the *Fluoroscope.* The wooden shoe-fitting machine stood four feet tall. He stepped to the lower platform and inched his toes into the X-ray box. Three looking glasses, like metal binoculars, positioned near eye level, peered down into the machine. The man flipped the switch and looked into his scope. He turned a knob until the needle on the gauge was in the correct position and then asked Jack and Gram to look into their assigned scopes. The three bent over the machine, their faces pressed to the metal frames like scientists peering into microscopes. They examined a green, glowing fluorescent screen with ghostly images of Oxford shoes wrapped around Jack's wiggling skeleton toes. The man affirmed that the boy had plenty of room to grow. Gram testified to the wisdom of the machine and paid the man. The two left the store and walked to a nearby cobbler to ask him to tack durable metal taps to the leather heels to extend the life of the shoes.

When summer reached its end and school began, Jack pulled his belt tight around the thick new denim that hugged his midsection. He reached down and folded the dragging cuffs. His toes wiggled in the stiff Oxfords that waited for a growing boy to stretch. Jack ran to school, his metal taps clickety-clacking on the pavement.

Jack at 12 years

Children in Jack's neighborhood played without toys. Each afternoon, young people of all sizes trickled out of their homes onto Fourth Street to play tag or football, to design obstacle courses, and to race. When it was time to pick teams, Jack stood waiting, looking like the inspiration for *Mad Magazine's* Alfred E. Newman. Jack's curly blond hair was cut short over his prominent ears, and his thick lips framed his slightly crooked teeth. Jack's skinny arms swung back and forth. His legs rocked side to side. He was the smallest and always the last picked for team play. Jack waited while the big-kid captains holding the football pointed to the neighborhood favorites, then the hopefuls, and finally the "scabs" to round out the teams. Jack imagined himself winning when he played. He ran his fastest, he jumped his highest, and he pushed himself to his childhood limits. He dreamed he was the finest on Fourth Street. *"Your time will come."*

The RCA radio advertized the wonder of Christmas each December. Boys asked mothers for new plastic airplanes, the exact models of the machines that brothers and uncles were flying over Germany and the Pacific, to replace the wood carved replicas that only pretended to be real.

Children could slip a paper reel into the Viewmaster and peek through its lenses into a three-dimensional world that took them to the faraway Eiffel Tower. When they flipped the lever, the disk rotated and they found the misty Niagara Falls. A new disk transported viewers across the world to an African safari where they stood facing a pride of majestic lions.

Christmas at the Yerman home, however, was practical. Irene searched the tree lots each Christmas until she found a small white fir with thin branches. She turned the tree with its best side facing frontward for Kathy and Jack to hang the painted glass decorations that Gram had collected over the years. Irene wrapped a pair of socks, a shirt, and underwear for her children and placed them under the small tree. Sometimes, she wrapped a toy—two years in a row Jack opened the same wooden plaything on Christmas morning, a wooden block with a hammer and six colorful pegs to pound from one side of a block to the other. Jack never played with the toy.

When Jack was ten, a strange gift appeared under the tree wrapped in the same green and gold paper as the socks and underwear, but this mysterious package boasted distorted bumps and peculiar twists and turns. It had a metal pipe, like a plumber might use, exposed at one end. Jack knelt to examine the package. He picked it up. It was heavy. He eyed the tarnished pipe and looked down its core hoping to find its secret. He could see only blackness. He squeezed the wrinkled paper. He felt the puzzling hard bumps and the contradictory spongy places. He smelled the mysterious package and sensed only the cool metallic odor of the plumber's pipe. Jack's anticipation grew.

"Mom, what is it?"

Irene sat smoking.

"Tell me!"

Irene blew smoke at the imaginary spot on the wall.

"Tell me, please."

She turned to her cigarette.

The week before Christmas seemed like a month that stretched into a year. No amount of prodding would get Irene to talk. The anticipated morning arrived. Jack hurried to the tree. His mother, sister, and Gram might have been there, but he saw only the package. Jack pulled on the excessive amount of tape and string holding the layered paper together. He loosened the metal pipe, pulled it out, examined it and concluded it was merely a deception. He stretched the clinging tape and a rock the size of an orange fell to the floor. It, too, was nothing. He tore the green and gold paper at its edges, advancing to the package's core. A spongy ball of holey socks rolled out. He pulled with his hands, elbows outward, and the paper gave way. A brown rubber Voit football fell to the floor and wobbled away! Jack's arms flew in the air, a happy squeal erupted, and he tackled the ball to the hardwood floor. He rose to his knees and then to his feet, sending a smile to his watching mother.

Mom looked back at her animated son, a smile hidden behind her pursed lips clutching the cigarette. She paused for a moment to say, "Now you can play."

Jack took his ball outside and found his best friend, Charles Foster, "Hey Chuck, I got a ball. Let's play catch!" They rushed to Irene's giant backyard. After a few overarm passes, Chuck decided to punt the ball. He held it in front of him, took a half step back, then forward, and swung his right foot upward. Chuck's foot connected squarely, sending the ball end over end, arching over the walnut tree towards the neighbor's yard. Jack ran with his head cocked upwards, watching the descending ball. He reached, but the football fell inches beyond his grasp. It bounced off the neighbor's barbed-wire fence and hissed the ominous odor of stale air. Jack held the limp ball in his hands and felt a lump of devastation in his throat. Chuck went home.

Jack returned to the house, tears building and beginning to roll down his cheeks. He held the lifeless ball out to his mother.

"I think it can be fixed," she said. "Take it to Cranston's."

Jack walked into Cranston's Hardware, past the paint, past the garden tools, and past the T-squares to the man in the apron busy behind the counter. "Excuse me, Mister," he said, catching the man's attention. "My mom bought this football here." Jack told his story about Christmas, Charles Foster, the kick, and the fence. "Can you fix it?"

Jack was too young to understand that eight years earlier, in 1942, Japan had strategically invaded the Dutch Indies and Singapore to control the rubber fields and 95 percent of the world's rubber market. The shortage plunged the United States into a crisis. Each Sherman tank's treads required a half ton of the precious rubber, and each warship had twenty thousand rubber parts (IISRP). Rubber had been a scarce commodity in the United States, so even after the war and with the development of synthetic rubber, fixing rubber toys had not been common to the people in Cranston's Hardware store.

The man took the ball, rolled it over in his hands, touched the tiny hole and looked back to Jack, "Kid, the Voit salesman comes to the store every two weeks. I'll ask him if he can do anything for you." Jack handed the ball to man.

The clock moved slowly for two weeks, but the news at Cranston's was good. The salesman had taken Jack's ball and said he would bring it back in a month. On the designated day, Jack sprinted to the hardware store. His Oxfords beat the up-tempo tap of a boy anticipating his second Christmas. Jack pushed the store's glass door aside and walked across the wooden floor to the man at the counter. "Oh, the football," said the smiling clerk, taking extra time to pretend not to remember where he had shelved the ball before pulling it from under the counter. Jack took the football, looked at it, and rotated it in his hands. He moved the ball closer to his face. It smelled like a new tire. Jack found a quarter-sized patch perfectly blended over the hole. "Thank you!" he said as he ran out the door and back home.

Jack stood in the middle of Fourth Street with the ball resting between his forearm and his hip just like the bigger boys. A football held peculiar powers in the fraternity of boys. It elevated Jack in the social pecking order. He was a bird with a bright feather, a reason to be among the young roosters who collected in front of their homes on Fourth Street or at the Beamer Park Grammar School playground. Jack had a ball and the boys would find him. He was now certain to play every afternoon.

"Jack, your time will come."

CHAPTER 2

Life's not Fair

[Jack,] I was worried about you because you seemed so depressed after the meet. No need for that; it was just one of those days when running was hard work for you. Every athlete has such experiences. The problem is to set one's teeth against these disappointments and carry on even more enthusiastically and determined for the races ahead. I know you will do this.

Coach Brutus Hamilton
(Hamilton, 1975)

Jack's introduction to injustice began when he was a year old. Irene had moved her little family to Woodland, next door to the Huberts. The Huberts had arrived in California as part of the great Dust Bowl migration from the South during the 1930s. After years of poor farming practices and a seven-year drought that sapped moisture from Oklahoma, Missouri, Arkansas, and Texas, massive dust storms consumed any hopes of making a living off the land. April 14, 1935, would be recorded in infamy as Black Sunday. A massive four-hour storm hurled choking dust and turned day into night while people huddled inside any hole they could find. It destroyed a third of the nation's wheat crops. At about the same time, California advertised for farm workers. By 1940, two hundred thousand people moved from the parched southern plains to golden California.

The Hubert family struggled to find food, water, shelter, and work, like so many immigrants in the Sacramento Valley. Farm laborers earned a dollar a day. Many of the landowners forced the Okies to pay twenty-five cents a day to rent a tarpaper shack with a dirt floor and no plumbing. Personal hygiene was a luxury and something the Huberts had learned to live without.

But the Huberts were fighters. They eventually worked their way to Woodland and settled on Fourth Street. Mr. Hubert built rickety rental cabins behind his house out of salvaged lumber, cardboard boxes, broken plywood, and tar paper. He filled most with relatives, and the Huberts grew into a herd of kids and cousins.

Jack remembers peering over the back fence at thirteen-year-old Peggy's "garden wedding," a notable social highlight on Fourth Street. The Hubert's yard was entirely void of vegetation and exuded the bitter smell of garbage and hardened dog feces. Peggy soon had three little boys of her own. When one of the boys was two years old, Peggy's husband rolled the pickup truck down the driveway without looking and backed over the toddler's head. The little lad was never quite right from then on.

Jack remembers Hallie, Teddy, Restoria, Peggy, Calvin, and Cecil. They were all a part of his growing up, whether he wanted them to be or not. One of Jack's first memories was standing on the street with the Hubert boys throwing pop bottles at passing cars. The Huberts had other destructive skills—they stole anything and everything. They took the vegetables from Irene's garden, the clothes off her line, and Jack's few toys. They stole his prized armada of miniature boats that he had crafted from halved walnut shells, clay, and toothpicks.

Mama Hubert was a corpulent three hundred pounds of rolling thunder. Her children could do no wrong. In contrast, Mr. Hubert was a cornstalk and looked twenty years older than his wife. His lower lip bulged of chewing tobacco. He passed the day spitting the sordid brown juice on everything, including the dog.

Hubert discipline employed a worn leather razor strap with a metal hook on the end. The leather strap was an inch wide and two feet long. It had once been used to sharpen a straight edge razor, but now its purpose was to beat Hubert children. Jack could hear screams for what seemed to be hours as they each received the father's whippings. This was the era when father was king, and Mr. Hubert imposed his imperial sentences as he wished.

Calvin grew angrier and more callous with each of his beatings. He was a mean and nasty kid who gained his family's respect and prestige by pounding on Jack. During the summer, the older neighborhood boys organized boxing matches and slipped gloves onto Jack's hands and matched him up against Calvin. Jack was small and certainly not much of a challenge. Calvin pounded on him to the pleasure of the cheering Huberts.

In the third grade, Calvin stepped in line in front of Jack at the drinking fountain. Jack tapped him on the shoulder, "You shouldn't cut." Calvin replied with a full-knuckle blast to the mouth and nose. Jack never had a chance to pull his hands from his sides. The teacher sent both to the principal's office.

Jack sat in a chair next to Calvin, blood staining the front of his only school shirt as he held a compress to his battered nose.

"Calvin. Say you're sorry to Jack," said the principal, "and don't ever do that again."

Calvin looked at Jack, "I'm sorry, and I will never hit you again," he said, his voice dripping with sarcasm.

Jack found friends in other places. The Hennigans lived in the poorest house on a poor street. It looked to Jack as if the peeling paint and random roof shingles held the frame of their one-bedroom home together. Like Jack, they had no father, but with twelve kids, there was always something going on. The Hennigans specialized in torturing small animals. They tied the tails of stray cats together and hung the frightened felines over the clothesline to watch them squirm and claw. They sometimes tied firecrackers to the poor animals.

Freddy Hennigan was Jack's age and dragged his clubfoot behind him, and they became friends walking to Beamer Park Grammar School. Freddy did not like first grade "readin', writin', and 'rithmatic," so he invited Jack to skip school. As soon as first recess started, Freddy headed for home and Jack followed. The two first graders ditched school for several weeks, but rather than going straight home, they travelled over fences, hid behind houses, and played in vacant lots over a route that covered ten blocks. They arrived home at about the same hour as if they had attended school.

The boys miscalculated their timing one day, and Aunt Gladys found Jack at home in his play clothes. "Why aren't you in school?" she asked.

"I've been playing with Freddy." Jack responded.

"Playing with Freddy," questioned Aunt Gladys, "during the day?"

"We leave after recess," explained Jack.

Aunt Gladys's eyebrows narrowed, "Are you telling me that you've been skipping school?"

"I think so…" whimpered Jack.

"You put your school clothes on, and we're going back right now!" she demanded.

Jack learned his lesson while Freddy continued to struggle. None of the Hennigans finished the sixth grade.

A few children in Woodland were fortunate to be invited to play in one of three swimming pools. One belonged to Dr. Nichols, another to the Cranstons, who owned the hardware store, and another to the Wrights, whose father managed the Spreckels Sugar Refinery. The Fourth Street kids rode their bikes in the three-digit valley heat and looked through the fences of rich kids splashing in the blue water and jumping off diving boards.

Learning to swim without a pool was a problem. Irene walked Jack to the Thompson Bus Company and stood him next to a red line on the wall. The line was necessary because the bus would take anyone who reached the mark to the university pool fifteen miles away in Davis. Anyone below the red line could not stand in the shallow end and might drown. Jack had visited the bus station for three years before his head hit the line. When Jack learned to swim, he took Mr. Thompson's bus forty miles to Madison, a little town in the country where a farmer had built a large pool. Jack could spend the whole day in the water for a dollar.

Back on Fourth Street, children played never-ending games of kick-the-can, football, capture-the-flag, hedge volleyball, and roller skating. Bermuda grass carpeted Jack's large backyard and became the Fourth Street field when needed. Down the street, the Zaragozas had a basketball hoop nailed to a tree. The Zaragoza brothers, twins Joe and Lollie, were the best at everything. Years later, they would be the stars of the high school basketball team.

The group played kill-ball in the street. Half the mob lined up at the picket fence on one side of the street and the other half at the hedge on the opposite side. When Joe or Lollie gave the signal, everyone ran to the football in the middle. If you got the ball, you advanced through the mayhem to the other team's fence. The other team jumped on you, pulled your hair, and cut you down at the knees while your teammates pulled the attackers off the pile. You never gave up the ball; it was a sign of honor! Even with the tackling, scratching, pulling, and pounding, the only serious injuries occurred when a player landed on Jimmy Henderson's water faucet.

This is where Jack learned to play ball.

Children followed World War II on the documentary newsreels that flickered from the movie house projector. A man's deep voice narrated the courage of American troops in the air, on land, and at sea. The Fourth Street gang reenacted battles using rubber-band guns for pistols. Each wooden pistol held four shots—one on each side of the gun, another on the top, and one underneath the barrel, all glued or nailed in place with clothespin triggers. Loops cut from old inner tubes served as ammunition. Jack would run behind a tree, take a shot, dive behind a bush, and launch a dirt-clod grenade into the battle.

Jack's back yard and the
Fourth Street Battalion with rubber band guns.
Jack's head is turned.

Jack was six years old when World War II ended. Then, something even better happened on Fourth Street. Everyone's brother, cousin, or uncle returned home loaded with army surplus. Kids chased each other around with Japanese swords, bayonets, German Luger pistols, signal flags, walkie-talkies, dummy grenades, signal mirrors, canteens, belts, hats, and uniforms. The Fourth Street Battalion, loaded with helmets, uniforms, and weapons, dug trenches and foxholes in Jack's backyard. The labor force grew, digging skills increased, and a new project was conceived. Thirty kids marched two blocks north to a vacant lot behind Darrel Hermley's house. The company of small soldiers, working in unison, moved tons of dirt. The ground gave way to tunnels and chambers. The regiment furnished the underground fort with furniture, electricity provided from extension cords, and carpets, until someone's parents investigated and discovered a missing living-room lamp. Neighbors summoned the city engineer, who inspected the underground fortress and called a crew of men with a dirt mover to fill the hazard.

Jack's neighborhood boundaries expanded as he grew older. His friends included the Owens boys on the next block, David Harrison, who lived two blocks over, and Norman Halden, who lived three blocks away, where the Huberts never went.

The day of reckoning arrived when Jack was eleven years old. Calvin hopped over the hog-wire fencing separating the back yards and sneered, "Jack, you're in trouble!"

As Calvin swung, Jack moved aside, grabbed Calvin's arm, and pulled him to the grass. Jack maneuvered to the left and wrapped his legs around the bully's torso. Jack squeezed Calvin's midsection in a scissor lock, reaching up and grabbing the boy's neck in a hammerlock. Jack's strength from biking and neighborhood games flowed through his powerful legs, and he squeezed harder, like a python sucking the air out of its prey. Calvin struggled for a moment. Jack saw the panic in his eyes.

"I'll get my brother!" threatened Calvin.

Jack hung on, feeling beads of sweat collecting on his forehead.

"Let me go! You're hurting me!" cried Calvin. "Let me go!"

Jack had waited for this moment for a long time. He smelled victory and tightened his grip even more. After nearly twenty minutes of squeezing, Calvin had no more fight left. He whined like a wounded puppy. Jack let him go. He had beaten his nemesis.

CHAPTER 3

To Tell the Truth

We are living in a victory-made, record-conscious time. There is a professional intensity creeping into interscholastic and intercollegiate sports comparable to the training of the professional ballet dancer. Some of this is good; some of it bad when it interferes with the more serious purposes of life; when it threatens to sow the seeds of moral decay into the lives of our young men and even into the lives of some of our institutions of higher education. Alumni and even administrators of some of our colleges want victory and some of them are not too particular how the material to assure those victories is brought into the institution, or what becomes of the young men after their competition is completed. "Yes, victory is great, but sometimes when it cannot be helped, defeat also is great," sang Walt Whitman. No victory is great when it is brought at the sacrifice of ideals; and no defeat is disgraceful as long as one does his best and follows the gleam of idealism.

Coach Brutus Hamilton
(Hamilton, 1975)

Twice, Irene bought three bus tickets and boarded her two children with sack lunches for a forty-five minute trip to Sacramento. Irene never explained why they took the trip, but it was exciting for Kathy and Jack to leave Woodland. The bus terminal was a block from the state's capitol, where Jack and Kathy played on the green lawns while Irene sat on a park bench smoking. She watched her children throw acorns at the blue jays and run after grey squirrels that darted from tree to tree. When the food was gone, the children followed their mother's silent lead. They folded their brown paper bags and walked back to the bus station for home.

Another family outing, more common, was to walk five blocks from home to the railroad tracks and watch the train chug through town.

Jack's shoes crunched over the grey gravel on the rocky bed supporting the track. He sucked in the oily aroma of creosote that oozed from the railroad ties. The tracks vibrated when the Iron Mountains approached, their bellowing horns announcing their arrival. The trains passed by, rumbling only a few feet from where Jack stood. He could feel the pounding reverberations in his chest, and his heart beat with the clatter of steel on the tracks. He watched the magical diesel engines pull, their bitter fumes tickling his nose. His mother watched with him. She seemed comforted by the mechanical harmony of power and steel. Jack waved to the man in the train. He wondered where the brawny metal cars had been and where they would go. He would have asked his mother, but he knew she would not answer. Irene looked down the long twin rails at the last car shrinking away. She turned, and Kathy and Jack followed her home.

Jack's classmates talked of driving through tunnels cut through the giant sequoias that reached to the heavens as if to hold up the sky. They talked of the deep blue water in Lake Tahoe. They wished to smell the fresh green forests hugging the shoreline. He imagined screaming down the wooden roller coaster in Santa Cruz. He wondered if the sand seeping between his toes at the beach would feel something like the spongy river silt near town.

Not traveling was hard on Kathy. She was pretty, blond, blue eyed, and was two years older than Jack. He watched his sister grow to adolescence and from innocence to trying to be accepted by the popular kids in town. The schoolgirls boasted of plans to soak in the sun at the beach over the Easter holiday. "My mother is going to buy me a new bathing suit," preened one of the girls who stood a little sideways, her shoulders turned back towards the group and her back arched, pushing her budding breasts further than they needed to go.

"Are you getting a bikini?" beamed Kathy, hoping for an invitation.

"Our mothers are thinking about it. We're going shopping this weekend," said the girl while the others smiled around her.

Kathy knew there would be no invitation, and even if there were, she did not have the money. When Easter Week arrived, Kathy spread a towel in the backyard. She massaged her reddening skin with sweet-smelling coconut oils and rotated from her back to her stomach, her white skin baking until she reached the perfect shade of bronze. That next week Kathy stood with the girls, her golden tan confirming fabricated stories of running in the sand, playing volleyball with the boys, drinking sodas, and cooling off in the salty waves.

Jack was eager to expand his world and told his mother that he wanted a bike. Two weeks later, a man arrived at the house with a large, faded blue bike. Irene gave the man forty dollars and handed the bike to Jack, but the eight-year-old boy could not reach the pedals. It sat parked against the backyard shed for a year. Irene saved her money from the extra shifts she worked and this time walked her son downtown to Ferrington's Appliance Store. There sat a glistening red Schwinn Ballooner equipped with a tank on the crossbar and a lamp on the front fender—the bike looked like a car. He sat on the bike. "It fits," Jack announced, and Irene handed the clerk the money. Jack rode his new bike home.

The bike was heavy, so Jack removed the tank surrounding the cross bar, its chrome fenders, the bell, and the flags that dangled from the handle bars. Jack's world increased thirty square miles on his new wheels. He peddled to Cache Creek five miles away to swim, or he pumped his bike the other direction to the warmer slough water. Jack would slow to a stop when he approached a farmer's freshly plowed field. He smelled the new soil and surveyed the soft furrows of uprooted dirt clods that beckoned him to a race. Jack dismounted, jumped the small irrigation ditch, and sprinted; he lifted his knees, denying the plowed earth the pleasure of pulling him down. The innate thrill of pushing himself to his childhood limits was electric.

Jack sits on the Schwinn Ballooner

Jack rode his bike to the Woodland Library, where his friend, the librarian, introduced him to Alexandre Dumas, the author of *The Three Musketeers.* Jack checked the book out, secluded himself in his backyard shed, and read. He imagined himself with D'Artagnan fighting alongside his three loyal friends. He wished to be as wise as Athos, as powerful as Porthos, as shrewd as Aramas, and as quick as D'Artagnan. He returned to the library and found *The Man in the Iron Mask* and later *The Count of Monte Cristo,* and read:

> *Those born to wealth, and who have the means of gratifying every wish…know not what is the real happiness of life, just as those who have been tossed on the stormy waters of the ocean on a few frail planks can alone realize the blessings of fair weather* (Dumas, 2010).

Jack's childhood resilience, and the still small voice reminding him that his *time would come,* compensated for his mother's emotional absence. One afternoon, Jack walked by his mother as she sat at the kitchen table smoking her cigarette. This time, she stopped him and burst out, "When you're eighteen, you're out of here!" She returned to her cigarette, and Jack thought, *OK,* and walked on. Eighteen was still a few years away.

Some weeks after Irene's decree, Aunt Edith, Loyd's older sister, brought her new husband from Nevada to visit. Jack bounced through the door to find Edith sitting at the kitchen table. She had dyed her graying hair red and was as bubbly as a young spring bride. She invited Jack to sit for a moment. She and the man looked at him and then back at each other as if they shared a secret.

"Jack, we want to talk to you," she said, her voice elevating a note. "You know, we're married, and we don't have any kids."

He looked at Edith and watched the grinning man sitting next to her.

"We are wondering if you would like to live with us and be our son." Edith had talked to Irene, who had told her, "If he wants to go, it's fine with me."

Jack was in junior high school and had just made the basketball team. "I like it here," Jack said as he slid to the edge of his chair, stood up, and hurried out the back door.

Jack liked Irene's sisters, who brought welcomed changes to his routine. Sometimes Aunt Gladys invited him to stay at her home in

Yuba City for the weekend, or Aunt Faye took him to the family farm in Nicolaus. Jack visited the farm two weeks each summer and again for a short time in the fall. He welcomed the early mornings and the invigorating aroma of freshly cut alfalfa. He breathed the sweet scent of garden corn. The dust from the walnut tree tickled his nose, and he loved the fragrance of ripening peaches that turned gold in the California sun. Aunt Faye had bird dogs, horses, milk cows, and cats; and Jack played with his younger cousins Mike, Bill, Marti, and Bob. He especially liked working with Mike, who could drive the truck and fix anything—including his younger brother Bill, whom he had once disciplined by hitting him on the head with a ball-peen hammer while babysitting. Bill recuperated by staying close to Aunt Faye in the house.

Jack grew older and watched the boys in Woodland paint, polish, and tune their cars for cruising up and down Main Street on Friday and Saturday nights. Cars in the 1950s were the size of living rooms, with large sofa-like seats. A "buck" of gas could fill the tank for the night. Teenagers packed into sedans as the sun set, and they synchronized radios to the Sacramento DJ spinning vinyl records. Some kids in cars smoked cigarettes, and everyone had a soda—the guys looked like James Dean and the girls like Natalie Wood.

Cars meant freedom, friends, and girls. Jack had mowed lawns, worked at the bakery, and cleaned a chicken farm, but he needed real cash to buy a car. The sophomore counselor called Jack to his office. The man looked up, adjusted his glasses, and said, "Leithold Drugs needs a clerk-delivery boy. The best part of this job is you get to drive the delivery truck." Leithold Drug Company had been founded in 1890 by J.V. Leithold and now was managed by his two grandsons (The Daily Democrat, 2011). "You need to go to the store and talk to the owners," instructed the counselor, "the Griffith brothers, Bill and Bob. They sell everything from food, to hardware, to camping supplies, and liquor."

Jack sprinted down Main Street, ran past the Woodland Opera House, and paused in front of Leithold Drugs. He pushed down his curly blond hair, tucked in his plaid shirt, and walked through the doors. Jack passed by the soda fountain with its sparkling chrome spouts where the soda jerk pulled levers to mix combinations of carbonated water, flavored syrups, and scoops of ice cream. The straws and long-handled soda spoons waited for the afterschool crowd that congregated to chat, laugh, and watch the alchemist brewing his magic.

The younger brother, Bob, welcomed Jack and invited him to sit on the red stool at the end of the chrome-trimmed bar. They chatted about the job and the work of delivering lunches to offices and medicines to homes. Bob asked, "I have an important question for you. We need someone this summer, but we also need someone after school and on weekends next fall. I need to know whether you will be playing football."

Jack looked at Mr. Griffith. He was a thin, handsome man with dark hair, kind eyes, and an easy smile. Jack wanted to work here—but didn't the man understand the importance of football in this town? Jack was in a quandary. He had been playing football almost every day since opening the strange package under the Christmas tree years ago. He wanted this job and the car, and if he said, "*No, I'm not playing football,*" he would be working and have the money for a car by summer's end. Jack could then claim to have changed his mind.

Jack looked at the polished red, white, and silver soda fountain. His eyes ran back and forth across the rows of tidy shelves. He watched the pharmacist in his white coat separating powders and pills with something that looked like a knife. He looked at Mr. Griffith, who sat waiting for an answer.

Jack confessed, "I'll be playing football." He knew this was the end of the interview.

Griffith looked at the boy. His mouth lay in a flat line rather than the easy smile he wore a minute ago, "I'm sorry, son. I would have hired you, but we need someone who can work afternoons in the fall." Jack returned home looking down at the passing lines in the sidewalk. He wondered whether he had made a mistake. "Should I have lied?"

Two weeks later, Jack received a phone call. It was Bob Griffith. The voice was energetic, and the words were urgent, "Jack, can you work tomorrow?"

"You mean I have the job?"

"Yup"

"I'll be there today!" and he *ran* to the store.

After several weeks of sweeping, stocking shelves, and delivering goods, Jack asked Bob why the change of mind.

Mr. Griffith explained, "We knew how much you wanted the job and understood that you could have lied about playing football. You, however, chose to tell the truth." Bob shifted a little in his chair and leaned forward, "We need good, honest people working here. We have drugs, liquor, and valuable items that are a temptation to someone who lacks integrity."

The Griffith brothers gave him all the summer hours he could work. The Griffiths had replaced the truck with a fuel-saving three-wheeled Cushman motor scooter, and Jack darted around Woodland like a superhero with his white pharmacy coat flying in the wind behind him. He delivered food, medicines, and the daily supply of alcohol to older women who met him at the door smelling like yesterday's bottle.

Bill approached Jack one evening with an unusual request. "Jack, could you stay and clean the store tonight?"

"Me? Sure."

The place was enormous! Jack pushed the mop between the shelves for nearly two hours. He hefted and hauled the galvanized bucket of dirty water to the large sink and poured the muck down the swirling drain. Between wiping sweat from his forehead, he wondered what had happened to the maintenance company that usually cleaned the store. Bill later shared that the president of the Woodland Chamber of Commerce held the cleaning contracts for leading businesses in town and had keys to many of the stores. The trusted president had been helping himself to anything he pleased. Woodland's police department searched the man's house and found radios, furniture, and kitchen appliances—thousands of dollars worth of goods. The president was not arrested, no articles printed in the newspaper, and the news was not broadcast on the radio. A few of the merchants and the police chief had gone to the man's home one evening and warned, "You have twenty-four hours to leave Woodland." Jack remembered the two teenage daughters—one of them had dropped out of the competition for Yolo County's Sugar Queen when her father left town.

The summer days grew shorter and the afternoon shadows longer. It was time to return to school. The fragrance of freshly cut grass and the symmetry of the white powdery chalk dividing the gridiron set the stage for the town's talk of this year's football team. It was the season, and the Griffiths gave Jack evening hours, after football practice.

Jack had earned a dollar an hour and saved every cent. Irene contributed an additional two hundred dollars, and Jack had the money to buy a car. He walked to the Chevrolet dealer in town. The salesman pointed him to a two-door '52 Chevy.

"How much?" asked Jack.

"It's $695.00, but I'll give it to you today for $650.00."

Jack looked at the car; he touched the rounded hood. He thumped the tire with his shoe. He sat in the driver's seat and adjusted the rear view mirror. "I'll take it. But you have to show me how to drive," he said. Jack had never driven a car.

Jack slid over, and the salesman sat behind the wheel to demonstrate the *three-on-the-tree* column-mounted shifter. The salesman moved the handle behind the steering wheel in an H formation from first to second to third gear, and then back across to reverse. The engine roared when he turned the key and pressed the gas pedal. The car was alive, and Jack's pulse quickened to match the motor's power. The salesman backed out and maneuvered the car through the lot, pointed it towards the street, turned off the ignition, and traded places with Jack.

This was Jack's car! Jack pushed on the brake with his foot and then found the clutch. He squeezed the smooth steering wheel in his hands and reached up to the chrome gearshift. He practiced moving his hand to first, then second, third, and back to neutral. Jack turned the key and the car ignited. The rumbling under the hood felt good. He put his foot on the clutch, shifted into first, and the car convulsed forward and jerked to a stop. The man told Jack he would figure it out, shook his hand, patted him on the back, and wished him luck. Jack proceeded down the road, sputtering the engine as the car bounced through the gears.

Over the next few weeks, Jack dismantled the car. He removed the chrome and "chopped the top" to make the windows smaller. He applied putty and sanded the corners to "mold" his ride to a smooth, rounded appearance. He added whitewall tires, full moon hubcaps, and skirts over the back wheels. Wires—curb feelers—stretched from the fenders to warn the driver of the road's edge. He added a *suicide knob* to the steering wheel, a ball-like attachment that turned the wheel. A driver had to be careful when the wheels snapped back into position and the knob flew around, potentially fracturing the driver's hand.

The car needed straight pipes and a "glass pack." Glass packs, sometimes called cherry bombs, were perforated exhaust pipes encased in a layer of insulation. A guy could drive by a girl's house, downshift, and send a reverberating message from the engine that he was out front. Jack did not have the money for the pricey modification, so he hammered holes in his muffler until he found a similar tone, but he soon discovered that exhaust seeped through the floorboards when the car sat idling. Jack kept his car moving to avoid this problem.

When all of the modifications were in place, he painted the automobile an eye-grabbing metallic blue-black. It was iridescent from one angle, and straight on it looked vampire black. Jack could ride with the best of Woodland.

On the way to school, Jack would pick up his best friend, Phil Persson. Phil and Jack's friendship dated back to the playground at Beamer Grammar School.

It was four years prior at this grammar school where Mr. Page, the middle school basketball coach, ripped Jack's shirt at the seventh grade basketball tryouts. The boys were running *the weave,* a drill where players pass the ball forward and run behind each other as they move across the imaginary lanes on the court. Jack had never seen the weave, and as soon as the ball hit his hands, he was bewildered, throwing it to the wrong person and running in the wrong direction. Mr. Page screamed at Jack, grabbed the boy by the shirt. Jack felt like a marionette under the coach's menacing grip and heard his Pendleton fabric tear down the back. The ripped shirt fluttered unnaturally. Jack's eyes filled with tears, but he remained at practice, crying. This was his only new shirt for the year.

A year later, it was Mr. Page who casually called out to Phil during recess, "Hey, you gotta come with me; your dad just died!" Phil froze in place—the basketball rolling away. "Come on, let's go," demanded Mr. Page. Phil's father had been crushed in a tractor rollover while working in the fields near Woodland.

Phil was a Mormon, and Jack had similar values. The fatherless boys loved basketball, neither smoked nor drank nor swore, and the boys gravitated towards each other to become loyal friends. Now with Jack's car, they escaped Woodland, making road trips to the Santa Cruz Beach Boardwalk, or beautiful Lake Tahoe nestled in the granite Sierra's and its pine forests, or to attend a San Francisco 49er's football game.

Jack and Phil in High School

Jack had earned D's in most of his high school freshman and sophomore classes, but as his discipline increased on the track and football field, his confidence grew; and as his confidence grew, his focus improved at school. He was strong and could run fast. People told Jack he could go to college, and maybe, because of his athletic talents, universities would look beyond his early academic years. Everything clicked his senior year when he earned all A's and he averaged nine yards per carry on the football field, but Jack tore a hip muscle early in the track season and managed only four races that year. He peaked at the State Championship with a 47.7 quarter mile—the third fastest in history for a high school athlete. Ironically, the two faster times were run in the same race, and Jack placed third.

During his senior year, Jack visited several universities on the merits of his athletic abilities. He was too much of an academic risk for Stanford. Oregon was impressed with his SAT scores but made no offer. The University of California at Berkeley was willing to take a chance if he attended summer school, which he did. Jack became a California Golden Bear. Jack's employers, Bill and Bob Griffith were thrilled! They were both Cal alumni and avid Blue and Gold fans.

The first Monday after high school graduation, Jack sat in class at Berkeley. Tuition was free in public universities, but the compounded expenses of food, housing, books, and clothing added up. Jack felt the pangs inside his chest when he sold the Chevy, but he had to focus on his studies. He performed well.

Jack returned to Woodland for a short break. Bill invited him to visit the store. The brothers asked Jack about school, football, and his plans. When the small talk waned, the brothers looked at each other. Bill pulled a white legal size envelope from his pocket and handed it to Jack. "This is for you," he said, smiling.

Jack curiously opened the flap, reached in, and pulled out a check. His eyes widened. He looked at the brothers, who smiled back. He read the words on the line. "Six hundred dollars!"

Bob noticed Jack's inquisitive look and explained, "It's a gift, as if you had worked every day this summer."

Jack remembered the day the Griffiths had interviewed him as a boy. He said a silent prayer of gratitude that even though he wanted the job, he had decided to tell the truth.

CHAPTER 4

Jack Who?

It's easy to see where a boy can suffer an athletic injury to his character.... From his junior year in high school he has been subjected to pressures and publicity. He has been led to believe that he can get something for nothing; that life is going to be all primroses merely because he can run or jump or throw or shoot baskets or evade tacklers.

Coach Brutus Hamilton
(Walton, 1992)

As a child, Jack lined up with the other boys next to the wooden utility pole that sustained electric cables strung across Fourth Street. He positioned his right foot forward, cocked, ready to sprint, and his left foot waited to explode from behind. Joe Zaragoza took the snap. Jack turned to cut back and meet the quarterback, who reached out and tucked the road-scuffed football into Jack's ready arms. "A reverse!" the boys on the other side yelled. Jack cut in; the cracks in the uneven pavement flew beneath his feet like chalk lines on the gridiron. The boys on Fourth Street imagined their names splashed across the newspapers: "Football Heroes!" The picket fences stood on the sideline cheering, "Go Jack!"

On the heels of 1952's fleeting summer, Jack reported to ground zero, the boys' locker room, the week before Woodland High opened for classes. Forty-five gangly freshmen stripped to their jockey shorts for the turn-your-head-and-cough physical. He stepped onto the metal scale; the doctor adjusted the balance weights and pulled the sliding T-bar down to Jack's head. In those days, the coaches assigned boys to teams based on age and size. Jack was five feet and three-quarters of an inch tall and weighed a hundred twenty-five pounds. The doctor wrote something on a piece of paper, handed it to Jack, and pointed him to the next station, where the coaches assigned him to the Midgets, the smallest of the groups. The trainer took the paper and exchanged it for a set of yellowing shoulder pads. Jack lifted the pads, examined them one way, breathed in the musty smell of fourteen seasons of adolescent sweat, turned them over, and looked at them again. *Which is the front?* Jack had no idea how to put them on. Frustrated, he dropped the equipment on the floor, exited the locker room, and walked home with his chin down as he kicked at the pebbles. *Maybe next year,* he thought.

"Martha" was not her real name, but it was what Jack called her because the sign read "Martha's Bakery" on the storefront. He worked at the bakery the summer of 1953, between his freshman and sophomore years. Martha was a large, rotund German woman with a pink freckled face, her hair pinned in a gray bun. She wore a white baker's dress protected by an apron spotted in a patchwork of stale bread dough and yellowing pastry creams. Work started at five a.m. Jack was surrounded by the heavenly aroma of leavening yeast, bread hot out of the oven, and the sweet blend of fruits, frostings, and butter. He swept the bakery's floors and washed the pots and pans, stopping only for breakfast—Martha had promised him all the donuts, buttery croissants, and warm pie he could eat. Jack began with a small tray of pastries in the corner, eating more each day, and over time, the small tray grew into a full table. Stuffed cream puffs and cold milk were Jack's favorites.

Jack kept his bakery money in a glass canning jar beside his bed. He folded the bills and pushed them in the container, and drew the coins from his pocket, adding them to the collection. Jack smiled as he watched his savings grow. He picked up the paper comic book he kept next to the jar, thumbed through the action packed pages, and stopped at the Charles Atlas advertisement. Mr. Atlas was the magnificent muscle man, smiling ear to ear and standing strong in his leopard shorts. The advertisement read, "I turned myself from a 97-pound weakling to the world's most perfectly developed man. And I can change your body, too!"

Near Mr. Atlas cowered Joe, his ribs protruding, and a sinister bully pounding on the scrawny boy. Joe's girlfriend, Helen, turned away in shame. "Don't let him hit you, Joe!" she pleaded.

In the next frame, Joe walked home alone and ordered Mr. Atlas's book.

Weeks later, Joe returned to the beach flexing his new and bulging biceps. "You're a bag of bones!" he shouted to the bully and leveled his rival with one punch to the chin. Helen, from under the beach umbrella, cried out, "What a he-man after all!"

Jack would be just like Joe:

Strong Muscular Body
Popular with Girls
New Handsome Looks
Bulging Arms & Legs
Success in Sports & Life

Jack found an advertisement for barbells in a sports magazine, filled out the order form, inserted his savings in an envelope, and walked to the post office. His P.E. teachers and coaches had warned, "Anyone who lifts weights becomes bulky and slow," but Jack ignored the advice. It made sense that he needed to be strong.

Anticipation of the weights stretched the four waiting weeks into a lifetime. It was like Christmas, birthday, and the first day of school all rolled into one when the crated box arrived at 122 Fourth Street. Jack found a hammer, pried open the staples, and organized the weight set in the back yard. He lifted every night. The strain on his muscles, coupled with blood pumping through his veins, invigorated him. He lifted until his calloused hands bled, but his body craved more, so he hammered a two-by-four across the shed door for a pull-up bar.

The weight lifting, combined with Martha's pastries and a growth spurt, helped Jack gain thirty pounds that summer before returning to football. This time, a confident young man walked into the locker room, and again the coaches assigned him to the small team. Jack looked at the shoulder pads, looked at the other boys figuring them out, and he turned his around, lifted them over his head, and dropped them over his neck like an old sweater. *I will play football,* he said to himself, *even if I have to play on the Midgets.*

Jack cherished the afternoons of running, catching, tackling, and blocking. He loved the warm breeze, the smell of turf, and running the ball. While the coach leaned against the chain-link fence and watched the varsity squad through the crisscrossed patterns of the wires, the young boys behind him played as if back on the street. Jack was faster and stronger, and the coach offered to move him to the B team. Jack declined, knowing he would sit on the bench when all he wanted was to play.

Through his junior year, Jack's growing body needed more calories than he could find at home. The pharmacist at Leithold Drugs concocted a thick brown mixture of peanut butter, coconut and soy oils, wheat germ and whey, the same high-potency potion prescribed to old folks at the rest home, and Jack drank one of these daily. The weight lifting, the pull-ups, the pastries, and whey shakes added hard muscles to Jack's lean frame.

In the spring of Jack's junior year, he ran the quarter mile in fifty seconds flat, faster than any high school student in Northern California. He had grown bigger and stronger and had proved himself ready for the varsity football team in the fall. The Woodland High team had exceptional athletes who, as young boys, had grown up running, jumping, racing, and tackling each other at Beamer Grammar School. As seniors in high school, Manuel Contreras could run the 110-yard hurdles in 14.2 seconds and drop kick a 40-yard field goal. Jack averaged nine yards per carry for a new school record, and several of his teammates went on to play college ball. Armand Jacques, Woodland's student body president, would go to Stanford; Ray Tolson became a guard at Iowa; Gerald Traynham was a tailback at USC, and Jack found himself at the University of California with high school teammate John Bogart.

The Cal freshmen played a three-game schedule against UCLA, USC, and Stanford. Jack stood on the sidelines for the UCLA game until the coaches called for him on the last play of the game. After the game, as Jack trudged alone up Bancroft Way, he thought of years of practice, effort, and sacrifices to play football. Emotion swelled within, and he fought the tears of disappointment as he approached his fraternity.

The next game, against USC, Wayne Crow was injured early, and Jack went in as a halfback. He scored three touchdowns, including a thrilling seventy-eight yard run. Jack's teammates patted him on the back, and his coaches seemed pleased. At the Stanford game, he was anxious to show what he could do against the cross-bay rivals, but Jack stood watching for the first half. He listened to the half-time locker-room adjustments, and he remained standing for the rest of the game.

Jack was confused, his disappointment returned, and he wondered whether he should play football next year or focus on track, but after several players failed their classes and dropped out of school, Jack's place on the team improved. He was on the California varsity team the following year.

Jack took pleasure in college practices as he had years before when he played on the Midgets. He ran the field, made hits, tackled, caught the ball, and felt the sting of sweat in his eyes and its salty taste in his mouth. He sprinted every drill to win and ran his plays hard. When the coach demanded push-ups, he did more. If teammates dogged in practice, Jack pushed harder. When he ran the ball, he pushed for more yards and hit the defense hard. He became an expert at running the opponents' offenses against California's first team. Maybe the coaches would see how hard he worked.

Jack Yerman, no. 41
University of California

California played Michigan State in its second game of the 1958 season. The pollsters had tabbed the MSU Spartans as the fourth best team in college football, and Jack planned on sitting comfortably in Berkeley, eating popcorn and listening to the game over the radio. He had no worries—until Wednesday—when the coaches called him over, "Yerman, you are going to Michigan." Jack was the third-fastest quarter-miler in the country, and if they could get the ball to him running around the end, he could turn on his motor for good yardage (Ives, 1958).

Thursday morning, Jack's roommate shook him awake, "Hey, they called from the airport and are holding the plane for you!" Jack had slept in.

"Uh-oh!" Jack threw on his clothes, grabbed his bag, and rushed to the coaches' frosty glares. He wondered why they had waited.

This would be Jack's introduction to the spectacle of a big game. He marched up the aluminum steps and boarded the piston-powered Douglas DC-6 airliner chartered for the football team. The athletes took their seats, the engines sputtered, and the props began to spin. The plane rumbled down the runway, lifted in the air, and headed for Michigan at twenty thousand feet. The "stewardesses" chitchatted with the boys; Jack helped himself to several desserts, smiled, and reclined his seat. Jack commented to a teammate sitting next to him, "I could get use to this."

The visiting California team practiced in an old field house made of massive interlocking wooden beams. In front of the facility sat a campus newspaper rack. Jack's eye caught the large block letters of the paper: WORLD TEETER-TOTTER CHAMPION VISITS MSU. Last spring teammate Jeff Snow had teetertottered 148 hours and 43 minutes without stopping (Maxwell, 1968). "Yes, indeed, we sure have earned Michigan State's respect," mused Jack.

The quarterback and co-captain, Joe Kapp, was the most celebrated player on the Cal team. Joe stood six feet and four inches tall, weighed a solid 225 pounds. Joe's future was bright; he would become the only quarterback in history to be an All-American, lead teams to the Rose Bowl, the Canadian Football League's Grey Cup, and the Super Bowl. Joe was already a big-ticket draw for this game.

Friday morning the press waited for the team. Joe walked onto the practice field to a clicking cacophony of cameras. The players nudged closer to Joe and smiled for a photo-op. One in the press shouted, "Hey, Joe, could you throw a pass?"

"Sure. Someone go out." Two fullbacks went in motion for a pass, one from the right and the other from the left. Neither wore a football helmet because, with Joe near, there was a chance of having your picture taken, and Mom, or your girlfriend, would recognize you in the newspaper back home. Smiling for the cameras, they cut sharply across the middle and *crash,* smashed into each other, their heads colliding like coconuts. Both fell to the dirt floor.

Wayne Crow, the first-string halfback, heard the commotion and rushed from the locker room. He stepped onto the field-house floor and into a drain hole. His body continued forward while his foot remained lodged and twisted in pain. Players and coaches surrounded the mayhem, trying to understand the confusion, and trainers rushed to the wounded like medics on a battlefield. Those with head injuries counted fingers held up in front of their faces, and soon, the three athletes had a bandage or a wrap covering a cut, a bruise, or a sprain. The bewildered coaches gathered for a short meeting, and Jack heard one of them ask, "Jack? Jack who?" Jack smiled and waved.

Buck McPhail, the backfield coach, approached Jack like a salesman, "Son, do I have an opportunity for you!"

"Yes," replied Jack, "I'm in the game tomorrow. But, Coach, I know only MSU's plays." Coach Buck reassured Jack he would teach him California's offense before the next day.

The team cleaned up and went to a John Wayne movie while Coach Buck, with a pad of paper and a pile of playbooks, met with Jack in his hotel room. The coaches had made adjustments, moving fullbacks to the halfback position, and assigned Jack to play fullback for the game.

As Jack looked over the scouting reports, one player stood out over all others on the Michigan State roster:

No. 88 SAM WILLIAMS ★★★★ 6'5" 225 lbs.

Sam had five stars by his name, was the highest rated player on the Michigan State team, was the team captain, and played both offense and defense. The Los Angeles Rams had drafted young Sam out of high school, but he had headed instead for Michigan State only to drop out and join the Navy before returning for his senior year

(Grinczel, 2003). This game against California would be the beginning of a tremendous football career for Sam. He would be named an All-American in every poll and become a twenty-eight-year-old rookie with the Los Angeles Rams before playing for the Detroit Lions as one of the "Fearsome Foursome."

The Michigan State stadium reverberated the passion of fifty-three thousand partisan fans. Hundreds of thousands more sat in front of their radios. Among them listened Jack's grandmother at home in Woodland who had never attended a game. He could not let Gram, Joe, or the coaches down.

Joe approached Jack: "If we win the coin toss, the first play will be a power right sweep. Do you know what to do?"

Jack had done his homework, "Sure, Joe. I know what to do."

California won the toss.

The play featured several options: The right halfback would split to the right, leaving the left halfback and Jack in the backfield. Initially, Kapp would take the snap and move along the line to the right. The right end would not block the defensive end, but slant for the linebacker. Jack's job, at 180 pounds, was to block Sam Williams. If the big man went for Kapp, Joe would flip the ball to the California halfback coming around. If Sam went for the halfback, Joe would keep the ball and cut up the field for good yardage.

It was the first play of the game and California had the ball. Thousands of Spartans chanted "Defense! Defense!" And, Jack was on the field. He looked across the line and measured his target. Williams looked even bigger than his description in the program. Jack backed up a couple of extra yards to build momentum. Joe called the count, the ball snapped, and Jack blasted for his collision with Williams.

That was all he remembered.

Later, Jack saw the film. Sam had refused to cooperate with Cal's plans. Not knowing what the Blue and Gold was up to, he crushed the Cal end behind the head with an arm blast, dropping the man to the ground. Big Sam turned to see Jack coming at him, head down at full speed. Sam put his arms together and ripped upwards, catching Jack under the chin and propelling him to a backflip. The California halfback had the ball by this time, and Big Sam, like a professional wrestler, picked him up, showed him to the crowd, and threw him five yards back down the field.

Jack felt a plangent pounding in his head and sensed the presence of people around him. "I think he's dead," a voice said. Another joined in, "Look at him bleed!"

All Jack could see was a distant beam of light. "What's wrong? Am I dying? No, maybe I'm going blind!"

The ringing in his head subsided, and he realized the circle of light was his helmet's ear hole. Williams had smacked him hard, splintering Jack's facemask, and the helmet had twisted half way around his head. The septum between Jack's nostrils tore, bleeding all over his new uniform. The referees called a timeout, maybe the longest ever in a college football game, because California had no more fullbacks. Jack had to be repaired.

The trainers worked their magic, the bleeding stopped, and they gave Jack a fresh jersey. He walked back onto the field, close to Williams so he could see what had hit him. Sam's massive arms hung by his sides. They were thick, covered, and Jack took a step closer for a better look. Sam had plastic sewer pipe taped around his forearms!

"Hey, is that legal?" Jack asked the ref.

Football players in the 1950s were experimenting with protective gear as padding evolved from thick cloth and leather to plastics. "You wouldn't want him to hurt himself, would you?" said the official as he looked away and blew the whistle for the game to begin.

California avoided Sam's direction for the remainder of a long game and lost 36–13. The University of Michigan, Pitt, and Illinois studied the Cal game, watching Jack fly through the air. They all had trouble from Mr. Williams that year (UPI, 1958).

Jack played sporadically throughout the season, but whenever the coaches gave him the ball, no one could keep up with him. The Sunday, October 12 edition of the *Oakland Tribune* dedicated six photographs and a third of a page to Number 41 and the final California touchdown in the victory over Utah:

```
[F]leet-footed Jack Yerman, the 440
star who plays halfback, crashed over
his own right tackle and raced 36
yards to a touchdown in the third
quarter yesterday at Berkeley. The
Bears finally won the game, 36-21. On
```

this play, as captured in the Tribune
Magic Eye photo here, quarterback Gus
Gianulius takes a handoff to fullback
Walt Arnold (1-2) and then gives it to
Yerman (3). Yerman runs by four Utah
tacklers (4) and is headed for pay
dirt. Utah quarterback Pete Ham gives
chase (5) but the speed burner goes
into the end zone (6) all by
himself(Oakland Tribune, 1958).

Hearts pounded a little faster, people stood a little taller, and
they leaned a little closer when Jack ran, broke a tackle, and cut
across the field. The campus newspaper, added:

[Yerman] is one of America's great
middle distance runners. His best
times are 46.5 in the 440, 21.2 in the
220, and 9.7 in the 100-yard dash….

Yerman's feats on the football field
this season have been something to
behold. He has carried the ball 18
times for 124 yards and a 6.8 average,
the highest on the team. Jack was a
letterman halfback in 1957, and
started at right halfback this year,
but injuries to fullbacks Bill Patton
and Walt Arnold forced coach Pete
Elliot to move Jack to fullback. And
he has responded very well at that
position….

He was selected Player of the Week by
the Daily Californian sports staff
after his fine performance against
Utah (The Daily Californian, 1958).

The Cal Bears dominated the Pacific Coast Conference, beating
Washington State, USC, Oregon, UCLA, Washington, and Stanford.

The coveted Rose Bowl in Pasadena, "the granddaddy of all bowl games," culminated the season. New Year's Day, 1959, one hundred thousand spectators filled the Bowl wearing California's blue and gold or Iowa's black and gold. The nationally televised game was set for two p.m. The mild Southern California weather added to the timpani of collegiate drums and fight songs filling the air.

Judy Crownover, Jan Smith,
and Margo Brown—behind the wheel.

Margo Brown, a vivacious brunette, her younger sister, Karen, and her Cal sorority sister and hometown friend, Jan Smith, sat among the throngs of students in the California rooting section. The girls had driven 120 miles from Taft to Los Angeles in the Browns' little blue Renault Dauphine—a car distinguished by its two horns: a guttural city horn and a shrill country horn. They had painted the California mascot, Oski the Bear, on the hood and rear of the car and joined tens of thousands of fans driving south over the winding Grapevine that connected the San Joaquin Valley to the Los Angeles basin. Fellow fans honked in approval at the girls, and the coeds honked their two horns in return all the way to Pasadena. The stadium's green grass and crisp white lines glowed from within the sea of blue, black, and gold supporters for California and Iowa. Margo pointed to a player, "Hey, there he is!" It was number 41, Jack Yerman.

The Hawkeye attack and the Winged-T formation proved too powerful for the smaller Golden Bears. Iowa prevailed 38–12. A disappointed Jack had played a token two minutes. Jack knew his time had come, and although football had been a childhood dream, it was not to be part of his future. The Rose Bowl would be Jack's last football game. Bigger and better things awaited on the horizon.

CHAPTER 5

A Good Bet

You now face three major decisions. First, the university which you wish to attend; second, the profession which you wish to follow; and, third and finally, the girl with whom you wish to share your life. I refuse, of course, to have anything to do with this latter decision in any case. However, I might say in passing that there is no dearth of charming, brilliant and high charactered girls on this campus, should you decide to cast your lot with us, and should you evidence an interest in such distracting items.

Coach Brutus Hamilton
(Hamilton, 1975)

Jack's eyes were burning. His head ached after three hours of studying. Berkeley attracted the brightest students in the nation, and Jack had some catching up to do. He set his books aside, stretched his arms to the ceiling, and walked downstairs. The "exchange," as they called it, between his Chi Psi Fraternity and the Sigma Kappa girls grew louder as he descended the stairs; the music from a Buddy Holly record on the basement Magnavox permeated the house. Jack headed to the fraternity kitchen for something to eat. There, he found his football teammate, Don Piestrip, animatedly chatting with a dark-haired and witty coed. She was drinking milk that Don had given her from the fraternity refrigerator.

She looked at Jack. "Hi, my name's Margo, Margo Brown," she said, tilting her head slightly and smiling.

Margo Brown

He shook her hand, "Hello, I'm Jack." He later learned that she came to the party as a favor to her roommate, Diana, a senior sorority sister who had been given the assignment to attend. Margo did not drink, and this event was about beer.

She recognized Jack, "I'm surprised you live here," she said.

"Yeh, me too, sometimes," he replied. The Chi Psi house was where book people lived, not a jock fraternity.

"I saw you at the track meet," she said. "You're the guy who sleeps on the grass."

Margo, a freshman, had followed track since high school and had attended Saturday's meet with her friend, Doug, who worked as a hasher in her sorority's kitchen. They had sat on the backstretch of the track where Doug said true fans sit. "Watch that guy down there," he said. "Can you believe that Yerman? He's only a sophomore and *man, can he run*! Look, he's sleeping! How can that guy sleep?"

It was a breezy California spring day, and Jack lay stretched out on the grass, seemingly unconscious to the activity around him while other athletes paced back and forth, fretting about the race. Jack had perfected the powernap before it had a name and slept until the call came from the loud speakers. He eased up, pulled off his sweats, and jogged to the starting line.

"Watch him," Doug said. "Yerman likes to come from behind."

Margo observed the sophomore's cool manner. Just as her friend had said, Jack made his move at the 220, caught the other runners at the 330, and won the 440 race.

Lively music wafted up the hallway and into the kitchen. Jack adjusted his black, horn-rimmed glasses. Margo noticed his movements. "I didn't know you wore glasses," she remarked.

"They're new," said Jack. "I don't always wear them when I run—I just wear them when I need to see!" Jack was running out of things to say, but he wanted the conversation to continue. "Would you like to dance?" he asked.

"Sure!" she smiled.

They navigated between people and made their way to the basement bar. She liked his jitterbug, and he liked her smile, but neither wanted to stay for long. "Hey," said Jack, "would you like to check out my friend Jeff Snow. He's in front of Bowles Hall trying to break the world teeter-totter record!"

"Let's go," she said, and the two escaped into the evening air, talking as they walked.

Some in Margo's hometown described the former beauty queen as "the prettiest thing to have come out of Taft since the discovery of crude oil" and "the reason desert wolves howl at night." Margo had learned kindness, charity, and prudence from her mother, boldness from her father, and poise from the countless civic functions she attended. She was intelligent, cheerful, beautiful, an honors student, and her calendar booked far in advance. Jack and Margo tried to set a second date over the next several weeks between his travel schedule and her busy calendar. The best they could do was an occasional bag-lunch together at the library or in her office, the newly created ASUC Publicity and Public Relations, where she would soon be director.

Jack's times on the track continued to improve. He was third in the NCAA championships, and Coach Hamilton suggested he run the open 440 at the 1959 AAU National Championship Meet in Bakersfield. The meet was only forty miles from Taft, Margo's hometown. Her parents, Bruce and Della, would be there with her to watch him run. "Oh, and be sure to take your passport to the meet," Coach Hamilton advised. "If you run well, you might go to Europe." Coach Hamilton, in his wisdom, had his top athletes apply for and carry passports. Having one could be the difference of making a team or not.

Bakersfield can be warm in the spring. Della fanned herself with the program. "There's your boy, Della," Bruce said as the runners congregated on the track.

"Which one?" asked Della.

"He's in lane three," said Bruce, pointing to Jack.

"Oh, Bruce, he's awfully old, isn't he?" said Della wrinkling her nose. Jack's thinning blond hair was cut short, so from a distance it reflected the silver rays of sunshine. Jack was nineteen.

The Bakersfield stadium was familiar to the Browns. A year prior, Margo, as Miss Kern County, had awarded the medals to the winners of national AAU meet. She remembered the first winner, a young black man who leaned over as she placed the medal around his neck; assuming she was supposed to, she planted a congratulatory kiss on his cheek. A meet official grabbed her by the elbow and pulled her aside. "Miss Brown," he whispered, "you can't do that!"

"Do what?" she said.

"Kiss the Negro boys," he said with some agitation in his voice. "It's not right—and some people will get very upset." His comments puzzled Margo, who did not carry the prejudices of the earlier generation, but she refrained from kissing any of the winning athletes from that moment.

"First call, men's open 440," the man announced over the PA system. Margo's thoughts returned to Jack, and Della stretched her neck to get a better view of her daughter's friend. The athletes congregated near the starting line. Bruce, Della, and Margo cheered as Jack ran and finished third.

Jack met Margo and her parents after the race and climbed with Margo into the backseat of Bruce's 1956 blue and white two-toned Ford Fairlane. The two-lane highway from Bakersfield to Taft rolled forty-five miles over the desert terrain. Jack would need to be back in Bakersfield by ten the next morning for a meeting, but in the meantime, he would enjoy the Brown's hospitality, Della's inquiries, and Margo's undivided attention.

Margo Brown representing Kern County
welcomes Vice President Richard Nixon.
Note the opportunistic politician (center)

Because Bruce measured special events by the quantity and quality of food, and because he had heard that Jack ate voraciously, he planned to be a gallant host at 410 E Street in Taft. Bruce filled every corner and recess in the refrigerator, which would have burst if it had not been for the latch holding the door shut. Jack awoke to the sound and smell of sizzling bacon and sausages. Stacks of pancakes, a platter of eggs, toast, syrup, and butter covered the Formica table while the refrigerator hummed with relief. After breakfast, Margo drove Jack to the Bakersfield Inn for the meeting. It felt good to sit behind the wheel of "Daddy's" car as they leisurely drove the two-lane highway and talked. They hoped Jack would receive an invitation for a summer travel tour.

Margo was familiar with the layout at the inn, having served as queen of a cosmetology convention some two years earlier. They sat in the hallway and talked while waiting for instructions. A man with the red, white, and blue Amateur Athletic Union insignia over the pocket of his blue blazer walked up to Jack and asked, "Is your name Yerman?"

Jack stood up and shook the man's hand. "Yes, it is."

"I understand you have your passport," said the official.

"I do," said Jack.

"Well, you will be leaving for Switzerland in two hours."

By now, Margo was standing as well, and she looked at Jack in disbelief. Margo turned to the man. "How can he? He doesn't have anything here. His bags are in Taft!"

"You'd better get his things, ma'am," he prodded and, turning to Jack, he continued, "We need to have a meeting in five minutes."

"I can be back in two hours…maybe!" exclaimed Margo as she pulled the keys from her purse and headed for the lobby door. She jumped behind the steering wheel and took off.

Margo crossed a series of four way stops on her way out of town. The car rocked each time she hit the brakes at an intersection. Each stop seemed to speak to her, "*You're not going to make it!*" Margo's frustration mounted as she reached beyond the steering wheel for the Fairlane's chrome gear shift. Her thought momentarily jumped to the car lot in Los Angeles where she had watched her dad haggle with the salesman about standard and automatic transmissions. "A man can shift a lot of gears for forty-five dollars!" Bruce said. She pulled the gearshift into first, her foot already on the gas, and the car leaped forward across the intersection.

She heard the unmistakable whine of a siren and saw the black and white patrol car in her review mirror. "Oh, no!" The flashing red light signaled her to pull over.

Margo's nerves were on the edge. Her plans for the weekend had changed suddenly, her folks would be disappointed, and Jack was leaving in less than two hours. She broke down in tears in front of the officer.

"Young lady, you know you're not supposed to be drag racing," he explained in a deep voice.

"Dragging? Who's dragging?" demanded Margo between sobs.

"You and that other car that's pulled over there!" said the officer, pointing to a vehicle that had also been detained.

Margo had been unaware of anyone else on the road. "I didn't even see that car," she explained.

"Miss," he said, "you pealed out pretty fast."

"My boyfriend's leaving for Europe in less than two hours, and he can't go unless I get his suitcase." Margo gave the officer the quick story.

Maybe because she was a former Miss Kern County, or because her father was a volunteer sheriff, or because of her tears, the officer paused, looked at Margo wiping the moisture from her face, and said, "OK, I'm not going to give you a ticket. You can go. Drive carefully—but you'd better hurry!"

She hit the accelerator, and a tail of dust lifted from the road's shoulder. Jack had phoned ahead, and Bruce was waiting at the curb with the suitcase in hand. He passed it to Margo, who climbed into the backseat while Bruce took the wheel, and Margo's younger sister, Karen, rode shotgun to watch for California Highway Patrolmen. Margo rummaged through Jack's clothing, selecting and refolding what he would take to Europe for the summer.

Forty-five miles later they pulled alongside the idling Greyhound bus with Jack waiting outside.

"Oh, thank you!" a relieved Jack said as he pulled the suitcase from the car.

"Do you have any money?" asked Bruce.

Jack looked in his wallet. "Three dollars," he said.

Bruce pulled out a twenty-dollar bill, all he had, and handed it to Jack. "Don't spend it all in one place!" he said with a smile.

Jack accepted the money, shook Bruce's hand, gave Margo a quick hug, and boarded the bus for LAX.

Jack had learned that he was part of a six-man American team competing in Europe. The world-class athletes included Ray Norton, the 100-meter world-record holder; Bill Nieder, the soon-to-be world-record holder and Olympic champion in the shot-put; Elias Gilbert, world-record holder in the 220 low hurdles; Bill Westine, a seven-foot high jumper; Tom Courtney, the Olympic 800-meter gold-medal winner and world-record holder; and Jack, the 440 runner who happened to have his passport. The six eager athletes flew to New York and then to their home base in Lausanne, Switzerland (Athletes Americains a Lausanne, 1958). The Americans would visit nearly every country in Europe and run a meet every two days before joining a full United States team for the first-ever track meet with Russia—behind the Iron Curtain in Moscow.

The rush of leaving California and Margo's family had left Jack contemplative. He had not expressed, in person, some things that he hoped to share with her. He liked Margo, and before leaving New York, Jack sent a heartfelt letter:

June 24, 1958

My Dearest Margo,

In the rush of leaving, I did not have a chance to say many of the things I wished to tell you. It is perhaps best that they were left unsaid until I see you again. I would only like to say now that knowing you has altered my life considerably. I find myself treating people with greater consideration and understanding....

After my hasty departure from Bakersfield, the team went by bus to Los Angeles, where we flew all night to New York and today have been seeing the sights and getting visas.

I think I know how badly you felt when I had to rush so last Sunday. You had looked forward and planned for the weekend, and you were hoping that we

might be able to enjoy ourselves
together. My brief encounter with your
family was short, and I hope that no
poor impressions were created.

I must apologize for this letter. I am
very tired and haven't slept since I
saw you last. I understand why the
Americans seem to fall short of top
marks on these tours.

The guys are a real swell bunch.

Love you always,

Jack

The Americans rarely lost an event in Europe, but without the
depth of a team, they could not stack up enough points to win a
meet. For example, the June 28 Lausanne meet program listed the 6
Americans and 113 Swiss athletes competing (Martin, 1958). This was
good for the European press. Newspapers reported victories as local
athletes, who finished second and third, compounded more points
than the Americans, who, when sober, usually finished first. Jack did
not drink and ran well most of the time. Back home, the newspapers
praised the small U.S. team:

ZURICH, Switzerland, July 2 (AP). U.S.
track and field stars whipped the rain
and the Swiss yesterday, winning four of
seven events in an international meet.

With most of the track under water and
the 4,500 spectators drenched by the
constant downpour, Jack Yerman of
Woodland, Calif., won the 400 meter
race in 47.5. Tom Courtney of
Livingston, N.J., the 800 meters in
1:52.4. Elias Gilbert of Winston
Salem, N.C., the 200-meter hurdles in

25.4 and Bill Nieder of Lawrence,
Kan., the shot put with a throw of
16.67 meters, 54 feet 2 inches.

Swiss athletes won the 200 meters,
110-meter hurdles and the high jump.

Ray Norton of Oakland, Calif., pulled
a thigh muscle and did not compete in
the scheduled 100 meters(AP, 1958).

At a meet in Lausanne, Jack promised to run the 800 with Tom to pace him to a new world record. Jack would take the lead. Tom would follow step in step in Jack's draft. At the appropriate moment, Tom would take over and sprint to the finish. Jack shot out of the starting block like a rabbit. He sprinted the first 400 with Courtney tucked behind Jack's shoulder. Jack could hear Tom's rhythmic breathing. He knew Tom was strong. At the 600-meter mark, Jack pulled to the side. To the delight of the crowd, Tom sprinted to a world-best time of the year at 1:47.9.

The American athletes became accustomed to the routine of unhurried parades, girls marching with colorful flags, and long speeches before the meet. The six young men chitchatted with the crowd, posed for photographs, and smiled all-American smiles for the enthusiastic Europeans. Fans collected autographs as Americans collect baseball cards. Young boys and old men surrounded Jack with treasured autograph books (Tonelli, 1958). Jack wrote to Margo and reported running in the rain and on muddy tracks. He described Switzerland as a "green and fresh garden." As any young man might, he took note of the lake near their quarters and was impressed with the bathing attire. He teased, "[The water] is too cold to do any serious swimming. I might say, however, that I am more convinced that you should get a bikini. The girls wear them, and the suits—they don't look half bad" (Yerman, 1958).

When the team boarded the train and crisscrossed the Alps to a meet in the northern Italian city of Milan, Jack was sick. He had been stung by an unknown insect while jogging in the woods. The bite had festered in his thigh to an infected battle of fever and puss. Jack could not bow out of his obligation to run, nor was quitting in his nature. He was scheduled to race against Panciera, the pride of the

Iberian Peninsula. While the other Americans were untouchable, the Italian had a fair chance of beating Jack.

The team arrived at the train station expecting an escort to the hotel, but found no one. Their ever-present Swiss host hailed two taxis and herded the team to a five-star hotel. After they had unpacked their bags, the athletes went off to see the city, leaving Jack in bed to calm his fever.

Jack's head felt soggy as he drifted in and out of sleep. The ache in his leg migrated to a pounding in his temples, which he eventually realized was a knock at the door. He got out of bed, limped to the door, and opened it to find a man speaking broken English. The man introduced Jack to a woman dressed in a white nurse's uniform. The meet directors had learned that an American runner was ill and had sent help. Jack welcomed them. The woman placed medicated hot compresses on his contaminated leg and gave him a shot of antibiotics. The attention alone seemed to make Jack feel better. He had hopes of beating the determined infection.

The boys returned from sightseeing to find Jack's spirits higher and shared with him marvelous sights of Milan: the world's largest cathedral, the masterpieces they had only seen before in books, and the delicious foods. While the athletes talked, they observed a persistent hotel porter who would enter the open door for a moment, look around, leave, and return to repeat the same routine. Bill Nieder, the street-smart, muscle-laden six-foot-eight shot-putter, was determined to discover what the impish fellow was doing. "On that guy's next visit, he's going to tell us what he's looking for."

When the mole returned, Bill cornered the man, who looked up at the towering athlete and noticed several battle scars across the American's face.

"What do you want in here?" demanded Bill.

The tiny man protested that he was innocent of anything but doing his job. To Bill, who thought little of diplomacy, the answer was not convincing. Bill grabbed the little Italian and carried him to the third floor balcony, flipped him over, and hung him by his feet over the traffic below. The blood flowed downward, and the porter's face reddened.

"I talk! I talk!" cried the tiny man.

Bill pretended to drop him an inch.

"I tell you what you ask!" screamed the man with greater urgency; Bill pulled him back into the room.

The Americans learned that big money had been wagered on the 400. The local Mafia knew that Jack was sick, and the odds had gone from three-to-one for the *Americano* to five-to-one for the *Italiano*. Gamblers tried to find any edge on the odds, and the porter had been hired to keep close tabs on any changes in Jack's condition.

Bill sarcastically smoothed the wrinkles out of the little man's jacket and sent the porter away. The stunned team looked at Bill, who turned to Jack and asked, "How are you feeling?"

"Better," said Jack

"Can you beat this guy?" Bill questioned.

The fever had broken, his leg was moving better, and the swelling had decreased. Jack, who was fundamentally strong, and with a couple of days until race night, replied, "I can beat him."

Bill turned, and with a growing smile said to the team, "We're going to get that money!" He called each of the boys by name and said, "Give me your money. I'm going to get it back for you, and more." He took the cash that each had saved from his three-dollar daily allowance. "Don't let anyone enter this room until after the race," Bill demanded, "and Jack, if you leave the room, you limp on that bad leg. When you warm up at the track, you limp again!" Bill pushed their money into his pocket and left the room.

The Italian officials hoped for the publicity of a big meet. A man approached the Americans during practice with a curious proposition: if Tom would push their ace 800 runner to an Italian record, the Americans would earn a trip to Rome. Courtney mulled over the offer. After thinking for a few moments, he agreed to the proposal on one condition. "I want to see the Pope," he said. The man agreed, but on the night of the meet Tom learned there would be no Papal encounter, nor would there be a friendly reception from the Italian spectators.

The gun sounded the start of the 800, and Courtney walked around the track waving to the crowd, who hissed and booed at the American. The temperament in the stands deteriorated further. Everyone, it seemed, was in a disagreeable mood for the 400-meter race. The restless mob surveyed Jack and argued over who would win. Some in the impassioned crowd placed bets. Jack could see the tattered Italian Liras passing from one person to another.

Jack sucked in a deep breath of evening air and smelled the freshly cut grass. His leg felt better, and he knew he had a respectable run in him. Jack pretended to limp, just as he had promised, and shuffled unevenly around the infield during the warm up as he surveyed the ruddy cinder oval. This would be a strange race. Rather than the usual 400 meters around two turns, this track encircled a large soccer field that swelled the track's oval to nearly 500 meters. The stadium lights focused on the center field, leaving the rounded curves buried in shadows. The runners would leave the light and enter the dark bend, only to emerge out the other side, having been concealed for a few seconds from the crowd. The race would finish with a 120-meter sprint in front of the heated fans.

Yerman on right, Panciera on far left

Eight runners were summoned to the far side of the oval track opposite the finish line. Jack knew exactly which lane the powerful Italian gamblers would assign the young American: number eight. Jack looked over his left shoulder to find Panciera in the choice lane, number four. The high-spirited Italian waved to the hopefuls, who would return home that night, brilliantly drunk, bragging of how they had made their money. In their eyes, Panciera raced for country and honor. The spectators leaned over the edge of the track to get a better view.

Like a calculating hawk preying on a rabbit, the Italian had the advantage of observing the American from the inside lane behind. Jack would not see the hunter until the final 120 meters. Tonight, Jack had a simple strategy. He would capitalize on the only advantage the track would give him, the unusual gentle curve of the swollen far right lane. Jack would hit the dark turn at a world-record pace and leave the unsuspecting Italian too far behind to make a move.

The athletes lined up at the starting blocks, set their feet with one slightly forward, knelt in position, and waited for the gun to crack. It fired, and Jack pushed forward as he had hundreds of times—but this time was different. The starting block blew apart into a confusion of pieces, and Jack stumbled to find his stride. Someone had tampered with the equipment. Jack could hear the runners and the spitting cinders from teethy spikes ripping into the track. He knew he was behind. Trying to recover, he pushed fast on the cinders, and they pushed back. Jack approached the dark curve, felt a surge of power as he hit the turn's obscure peak, but disaster hit again. Jack felt a sharp pain shoot up his leg as if a bullet had been fired from the ground, cutting through his calf into his pulsating thigh. His leg gave out—body flinging forward—as the horizon moved perpendicular. Jack instinctively ducked his head, rolled over his shoulders in a flying somersault, and returned to position without losing a step! It was a move he had learned years before from Robert Allen, a grammar school football coach, and Jack was upright just in time to see Panciera pass him as they reemerged into the light. The Italian had a ten-meter lead with 120 meters to go.

Jack's adrenaline surged. Every sense heightened, his vision clearer, his running sleeker, and he exploded after the Italian. He sprinted off the curve to the final straightaway at the feet of the maniac crowd that pelted him with food and rubbish reeking of alcohol. Jack focused on Panciera with the vindictive instinct to win. The hunted was now the hunter. Three meters, then two, one—the crowd screamed. He heard Bill yell something. Jack leaned forward at the tape and won by inches. Jack was clocked at a world-class time of

46.8 on an unusual track. Panciera was right behind at 47.7 (Dessena, 1958). The disappointed fans quieted.

What happened on that turn? Jack brushed the dusty cinder off his jersey and walked back to the dark curve. His eyes adjusted to the shadows as he bent down to feel the track. There they were—a cluster of malicious round holes strategically dug four inches deep in his lane. The holes were invisible in the dark cinder. He could have broken his ankle or blown out his knee and ruined his career.

The following day the team boarded the train for Switzerland. Bill was talkative and cheerful, but neither Jack nor any of the other athletes ever saw their money.

CHAPTER 6

To Russia with Love

I hate to see sports used in a kind of political propaganda and I hope that our own country can remain civilized enough never to stoop to this.

Coach Brutus Hamilton
(Hamilton, 1975)

The world was frightening and unpredictable in 1958. The United States and Russia were at the height of the Cold War, and the United States set the rules for a dangerous game: *We have the bomb and you don't. If you don't do what we say, we get angry and drop our bomb on you.* The Soviet Union soon joined the game and tested a big bomb of its own. Now, the game was more complex: who could make the biggest "boom"? The United States exploded a nuclear weapon and Russia responded with one bigger and better. The bombs grew fatter. The US blew holes in the bottom of the Pacific Ocean, and at one point, disintegrated an entire island. The Soviets responded by firing a bomb into the stratosphere so powerful it would have blown a hole a mile deep and five miles round if on Earth. Russian military shot at American pilots taking secret photos over Soviet air space. In two more years, the Soviets would bring down U-2 pilot Francis Gary Powers, who would sit in prison until a dramatic exchange was arranged for the Soviet master spy Colonel Rudolf Abel, who had set up a spy network in New York City. Brinkmanship, the policy of pushing a dangerous situation to the brink of disaster, had set humanity on a catastrophic collision course.

President Eisenhower and Premier Khrushchev signed a *détente*, a French word meaning, *Let's relax a little and pretend to be friends.* Governments in both countries had fed people misinformation, and as a result, the Americans and Soviets were ignorant and afraid of each other. Some hoped that cultural exchanges might help the superpowers become a little friendlier. With *détente*, Stalin's Iron Curtain would open for the first time. Dark-suited diplomats in far off places discussed exchange options: the Russians wanted the American track team, and the Americans asked for the renowned Bolshoi Ballet. These were the circumstances that led to Jack's participation as one of the youngest members of the first American team to penetrate the Iron Curtain.

As a member of the small American team traveling through Europe, Jack, at age nineteen, had lived a celebrity summer competing in remarkable cities, tasting new dishes, and signing autographs. During that same period, the U.S. national team had spent much of the torrid summer waiting at West Point, confined to a routine of tedious training and wondering whether the Soviet meet would happen. "How would the Soviets use the event to their advantage?" "Would the Americans be safe?" At the last moment, the dark-suited men decided that it would look bad for Moscow if the track team could not compete (AP, 1958).

Officially, the U.S. team was seventy-three strong, including the coaches, and was the largest delegation of American track-and-field stars ever assembled outside the Olympics. The team included six previous Olympic gold medalists (Marannis, 2008). The Soviet press reported that the meet was sold out—104,000 spectators would fill the stadium, and the Russians would not discredit themselves by demonstrating against the United States at the meet.

Jack's small touring team met the U.S. national team in Helsinki. Instead of the seventy-five athletes and coaches he had expected at the airport, there was a sea of two-hundred people waiting to board the three planes. "Why such a large group?" Jack asked one athlete. He was told that many were government officials—State Department and trade officials, likely including CIA, some piggybacking on the team to gain entry into Russia.

The team waited all day at the airport. When Jack asked why so long, the answer came back, "The Russians want us to arrive after dark." The sun descended to the horizon with hints of orange and purple peaking through the evening clouds. A small fleet of planes sat at military attention with wings staggered in formation and bellies open, awaiting the American athletes. These were not the modern jets that Jack had expected, but Russian *Lisunovs*—small, twin-engine tail-dragging imitations of the American fat-bellied DC-3 workhorse.

The Russians would not allow American aircraft over Soviet landscape, just as anxious Americans feared Aeroflot overhead.

These young athletes were America's pride, and possibly the most talented track team ever assembled—an army of crusaders sent to proselytize democracy in well-pressed charcoal-grey travel slacks and smart-looking skirts, white-collared button down shirts for men and matching blouses for the women. Jack's narrow red, white, and blue tie fluttered in the gentle breeze as he stood waiting with his blue USA sports bag at his side. The officials announced that it was time to board the planes; former Olympic athletes, world-record holders, and officials to the front, and others, like Jack, found themselves in the last group. He walked to his assigned plane, stepped from the tarmac, and ascended the metal staircase. The barren interior reminded Jack of an old Bluebird school bus with stiff, upright seats. He chose a seat near the entrance, thinking a quick exit might be beneficial if the engines failed.

The planes lined up and took off one by one. "Last on" means "first off," so Jack's plane led the squadron of metallic birds over the Russian landscape. As the ground drifted away, Jack felt uneasy, thinking of the young American soldiers who only days before had stormed Lebanon's beaches to restore stability to that troubled country. "American Colonialism" brought heated responses from the communists who had organized angry demonstrations for the world to see. Jack wondered how the team would be received in Moscow.

From his bird's-eye view, Jack watched grass-roofed barns flowing under him. He saw an occasional farmer working his way home before nightfall, and he could almost see the definition of each shingle on the country homes. Jack soon understood the reason they had been crowded into the old planes. The Russians, who controlled the route and altitude, had been careful to prevent the Americans from taking photos of anything significant. Dusk faded into night, and the Soviet pilots maneuvered the planes towards rows of kerosene torches held by soldiers signaling the outer limits of freshly graveled runways built for refueling on this trip. Young soldiers hurried from the shadows, rolling fifty-five gallon drums, and hand-pumping fuel into the thirsty planes.

The fleet approached Moscow, a city of six million people. Jack's plane hit the tarmac and taxied to the hangar, and the pilot opened the door. Jack unfolded himself from the plane, stood in the doorway, and breathed the summer night's air. He looked for the other planes with the Olympians and diplomats, but they were nowhere to be seen. It occurred to him that he would be the first American the Soviets would meet, and he felt it his duty to represent his country and team. He descended the steps, lifted his right arm, and waved to the gazing Russians with his all-American James Dean smile. Two beautiful girls approached, reminding Jack of USC cheerleaders, except for their white blouses, knee-length plaid skirts, and lacy cottage aprons. The girls placed an abundant bouquet of fragrant flowers in Jack's hands. The blond girl leaned over and kissed him on the cheek. He felt his face flush and his heart thump.

The blond girl spoke English with a crisp British accent, introduced herself, and explained she was studying tourism at the University of Moscow and worked for *Intourist*, the official state travel agency. Jack later learned that *Intourist* was founded in 1929 by Joseph Stalin and staffed by KGB officials, and would grow to be the largest travel agency in the world (Chong, 2006). The agency managed foreigners' access to and travel within the Soviet Union. The blond girl stopped for a moment, looked around to affirm that she would not be heard by others, lowered her voice, and whispered to her new American friend, "Do you believe in God?"

Jack looked at her curiously, "Yes, I believe in God," he said, realizing at that moment her question sprang from the state of affairs in the USSR. Lenin had once said that religion was the opiate for the people, a spiritual booze (Lenin, 1905), and to believe in God, in Russia, was for the old and unsophisticated.

The blond girl looked around again and then turned to Jack, "Do you live in a cottage?" In her world—the Moscow that Stalin had built—a private home, even a small cottage, would be a luxury. The city's masses lived behind a monotonous blend of repressive cement apartments where mothers, fathers, children, neighbors, newlyweds, the old, the sick, the strange, and the innocent shared kitchens and bathrooms for the benefit of the State. As Jack would soon learn, duplicitous doormen, often women, held all the keys to the apartments and kept watch, signing tenants in and out. They noted in their books the arriving rations of meat, vegetables, flour, and cooking oil, even a small piece of cake delivered to a cherished grandmother. Nothing was private.

Jack thought about his childhood and home on the other side of the world…

Mom, Gram, Kathy, and Jack had all shared the same bedroom. Jack had slept in the baby crib until he was six, and then, for a time, shared the bed with his sister at night—the same bed where Mom slept during the day. As the children grew, Jack needed his own space away from the women. He converted the eight-by-ten-foot slat-board shed in the backyard to a bedroom.

Fixing the Roof on Jack's Backyard Shed

He had pushed his bed to the low end of the sloped ceiling, crammed rags in the knotholes to slow the penetrating cold from the damp winter, covered the walls with newspaper, repaired the roof, and slept under layers of blankets. It was *his* cottage, a space where he could dream, think, read, and grow more confident until he left for the university. Jack was unexpectedly overwhelmed that his humble home would be a luxury in Moscow. "Yes, I live in a cottage," he said.

The aircraft carrying the Olympians and the diplomats arrived. The group boarded the waiting buses and headed towards Moscow's evening lights. Russia had not opened its doors in decades. The American athletes were the first significant group to be welcomed at the capacious Leningradskaya Hotel, an enormous facility reaching to the sky with hundreds of empty rooms. The bronze lattice entrance, the carved-timber ceilings, the chandeliers, and the lion sculptures could not hide the hasty construction. The travel-weary Americans expected prompt service and room assignments, but the unpracticed Russians were not prepared for a crowd. In the confusion, Jack was the only athlete assigned to a room on a floor separate from the rest of the team. Everyone else was assigned to the floor above.

Jack went to his room, laid his tired body on the hard mattress, and thought of home. Woodland was like other small towns in the United States where children watched newsreels and TV warnings of radiation maps and potential mass destruction. Children practiced duck-and-cover drills at school. Evacuation signs marked the quickest routes out of the big cities. City councils designated cement basements in town halls and libraries as safe zones, and Middle Americans built fallout shelters of their own. Jack shut his eyes and resolved he would be an exemplary American. As Jack drifted to sleep, he considered that he might personally prevent World War III by making a Russian friend.

The athletes had five full days before the meet. Much of that time was spent dozing in the hotel or training while the Russians filmed the American workouts (Marannis, 2008). The Americans began to explore Moscow. On the way to Lenin's tomb, Jack made sure to smile warmly and talk to everyone, but it was difficult to have a conversation even though crowds followed the team trying to speak English. "Hellow, jou look like a Russian," some would say, but a conversation was not what they wanted. They simply hoped for a reply.

The Americans began to drift all over Moscow, and Jack still needed to make a friend. He decided the best option to unite the Russian and American worlds was to befriend the *dezhurnaya*, his maid, with the keys, who sat at a desk in front of the elevator on his lonely floor. She was the epitome of an ageless, wrinkled Russian grandmother, standing a little more than four feet tall with beady gray eyes and a little bun on top of her head. Each time Jack walked to his room, she handed him his key attached to a heavy steel ring attached to a solid metal ball.

Even though he smiled his biggest smile and said *"Da"* to the Russian key keeper, she did not respond. *Maybe she's afraid of me,* he pondered. People in the Soviet Union lived in fear of the KGB, with its secret operatives, masters of disinformation, torture, and assassination. Jack ran into Russian fears when he and decathlete Rafer Johnson attempted to shoot home movies with an 8 mm camera. When the Americans walked to the market, Rafer lifted his camera only to be met by a fist-shaking crowd that turned on the Americans and shouted angry words in Russian. Later, Jack tagged along with hurdlers Ancel Robinson and Hayes Jones to a neighborhood of dilapidated row houses that dated back to the turn of the century. The residents surrounded the athletes, and one angry man, in broken English, demanded, "No photos!" The Russians seemed ashamed of their paucity and did not trust the American visitors. The athletes retreated, and Jack had yet to make a friend.

The team visited GUM, on Red Square, the oldest department store in the world. To an American who could shop at Woolworth's or Sears, this place was barren. GUM reflected the dearth of the Russian Five Year Plans, which explained why Jack had been approached several times by people offering fifty dollars for his used Levi's. In the midst of this meagerness, Jack realized he could bring some joy to his maid's lean and colorless life by showing the souvenirs he had collected from all over Europe. No doubt she would be fascinated with his little trinkets, perfume, silks, toys, and glass. Jack decided he would place a map on her desk, point to the places he had visited, and if he gave her a gift, he would make a friend.

Jack collected the trinkets from his room and set them one by one on her desk next to the map. The Russian grandmother responded with *"Da, da,"* but was not enthusiastic. "Maybe she's a little frightened," thought Jack. "This isn't going to be easy."

Jack had another idea. While visiting the U.S. Embassy commissary, he had bought rootbeer, peanut butter, and cashews. Jack left the map on her desk and ran back to his room. "She is going to have the treat of her life!" He grabbed the can of cashews and sprinted back to Grandma Russia's desk, with the nuts clanging up and down in the can. When Grandma saw the streak of red, white, and blue racing towards her, her beady black eyes widened. She reached for the collection of keys, and took off in the opposite direction. Jack shifted gears to race pace and chased after her. Her low center of gravity gave her the advantage—she was moving fast, her keys jangling, and Jack pursuing her with cashews rattling in the can. She hit the doorway and disappeared. By this time, Jack stopped his pursuit and laughed, "This is my first race behind the Iron Curtain, and I lost!" He returned to his room, opened the can of nuts, breathed in the scent of sweet cashews, and ate a few in her honor. He pulled off his sweats, collapsed in his bed, and slept.

Somewhere, when sleep was at its deepest, when the body was at its most gratifying rest, long before the sun rose—*Bam*—Jack was thrust awake by silhouetted invaders brazenly crashing through a now wide open door. Blinding lights seared his blinking eyes as he pulled into focus the pointed barrels of a pair of Russian automatic rifles. The squarely dressed, uniformed major barked, "Jou are vunder arrest for attempting to assault jour maid!"

Assault? Am I going to be shot? Jack was bewildered. The soldiers pushed their guns into the American. He saw the pear shaped woman glaring from behind her brigade—clutching the keys in her fat little hands.

The major peered at Jack, back at her, and then back to the American. The soldier's lips curved to a smile for a moment and then back to his serious form. The major belted, "Impossible! But jou vill come vith us." Jack pulled on his sweats, and the soldiers marched him to the end of the hall and through the exit. Their army boots pounded up the steel staircase to the U.S. team's floor, advanced down the corridor, and stopped in front of a door. The old woman followed along, shifted her keys, and found one to fit the lock. She turned the pins and opened the door. The soldiers threw Jack's belongings inside and motioned for him to enter, "Jou vill stay here."

It was dark. Jack smelled the semisweet acrid sweat of a well-seasoned athlete. He hesitated for a moment, flipped the switch, and the light fell down the walls, across the twin beds, and over his scattered belongings. This room belonged to Harold Connelly, the 250-pound, handsome, gregarious world-record hammer thrower.

Harold was not a man who understood the word "no." His tenacity began at birth. At twelve and a half pounds, he set the record for the heaviest baby born at Somerville Hospital in Massachusetts, but his size made delivery difficult. He dislocated his left shoulder and crushed his brachial plexus nerves at birth. Harold fractured his feeble left arm thirteen times as a child, and consequently, it grew to be four and a half inches shorter than his right, and his left hand two-thirds the size (HammerThrow.org). Harold would say, "They didn't treat the disabled with dignity then. I couldn't stand to be treated differently.... The thought of being patronized made me sick. I wanted to play by the rules, not rules adapted for me because I was disabled" (Litsky, 2010). Like Jack, Harold had discovered weight lifting in his early teens and that it would help him overcome his weakness. Harold had soon excelled at the shot put and football in high school. He attended Boston College and volunteered to help the hammer throwers retrieve hammers. "Before long, Harold was throwing the hammers back to the teams' throwers farther than their throws into the field" (HammerThrow.org).

The hammer is a symbol of strength, coordination, and agility. The athlete propels a sixteen-pound metal ball attached to a handle by a four-foot-long chain. The thrower spins three or four times in a ring and flings it. What Connolly lacked in arm strength, he made up for with speed and leg power, and when he won the gold medal in Melbourne, 1956, photographers yelled to him to raise his arms in victory. Harold lifted only his right arm (Litsky, 2010).

Harold met beautiful Olga Fikotová, the Czechoslovakian Olympic discus champion and the pride of the Soviet Block, in Melbourne. The talented youths talked and spent time together at the Olympic Village. Harold spoke to Olga in fragmented German, and she responded to him in broken English. Their curiosity developed into friendship, and their friendship into romance (Willoughby, 2008).

Connolly proposed marriage a few months later. The Cold War relationship between two gold medalists could not have been more complicated and required diplomatic intervention. The U.S. Secretary of State, John Dulles, announced at a press conference, "We believe in love," but the Czechoslovakians were less willing. Olga would later share, "It was unheard of at the time, and the [Czech] government didn't know what to do with it. They rather unpleasantly told me what they thought about being a traitor" (The golden girl, 2006). Harold suggested that they both write a letter to President Antonín Zápotocký. The president granted Olga an audience and warmly received the Olympic champion. As they talked, he cautioned Olga that that if she were to go to the West, she would forget her country and "sell out to the American glitter" (Duguid, 2012). Olga loved her homeland and explained she would honor country and continue to represent Czechoslovakia in sport. She simply was in love with another athlete who happened to be an American and requested permission to marry.

President Zápotocký listened and said, "I cannot help very much, because different offices make the decisions. What do you want me to do?"

"Just do whatever you can," responded Olga. "If you can put in a kind word, I'd be most grateful."

"I'll tell you what," said the president, "you have my blessing, and I'll put in a word for you" (Willoughby, 2008). A few days later, Olga received a permit to marry a foreigner.

Harold visited Prague in 1957 following a European goodwill tour for the U.S. State Department. The two planned a quiet wedding in the middle of a week, hoping to stay under the radar of the authorities and to protect her parents from the negative attention (Willoughby, 2008). In spite of their efforts to keep the ceremony a secret, word got out, and thirty thousand people turned up in the town's square to celebrate. "People sang and cheered and walked along with our wedding party," recalled Olga. "When the Prague police officers smiled and waved and asked people to let us walk through, I realized this was an extraordinary moment" (Duguid, 2012).

The Czech government issued permission for Olga to emigrate to the United States. Harold sold one of his hammers to buy tickets, and Olga travelled with a government issued paper of official signatures and bureaucratic stamps. She realized something was wrong on the express train to Vienna when, at the border, everyone had a passport. Olga knew little about travel documents and never had travelled with a passport. The controlling Communists had always carried their athletes' documentation to prevent defections to the West.

When the newlyweds arrived in the United States, they reported to the Czech embassy in Washington to meet the ambassador and regularize Olga's paperwork. Olga intended to keep her promise to the president and represent her country at the European Championships. She assumed that she would exchange her official paperwork for a proper passport and a visa. When she explained her predicament and handed the paper to the ambassador, he looked at it, paused, sat back in his chair, and glared at the young athlete. "We do not expect you to traipse around the world," he said (Willoughby, 2008).

Olga sat stunned as she realized that without a passport she would not travel and could not keep her promise to the president.

It was Harold's turn. He took advantage of the trip to Moscow, the control center of the Soviet Union, to obtain a visa for Olga; and now, Jack was in Harold's room. Jack did not know that there were wires embedded in the plaster carrying noise through the hotel's walls and back to Soviet ears. Unseen listeners heard Jack wonder out loud, "Where's Harold?"

The sun's warm rays announced morning through the window. Jack rolled over, opened his heavy eyes, and looked across to Harold's untidy bed. The big man was still missing. He sat up, rubbed his face, and cleared his senses in time to welcome a heavy, square woman, barging through the door, yelling and pointing at Jack's mess on the floor. The woman abruptly turned and exited, leaving Jack scratching his head. A few minutes later the same woman returned, followed by Dan Ferris, the chairman of the U.S. Amateur Athletic Union, and an interpreter. Dan looked over the scene while Jack explained that he had just been trying to make a friend with a can of cashews before the ruckus started.

Dan listened, looked at the clothes on the floor. "Jack, it's absurd, but just go along with them," he said, shaking his head. Jack picked up and folded his clothes, found places in the drawers and closet, and even made Harold's bed.

After breakfast, Jack headed for his workout at Lenin Stadium. He walked by the corner where the bulky weight men hung out. A friendly arm grabbed him. It was Harold. "Comrade Yerman, you're my new roommate!"

"Yeah, Harold, it's been crazy. Where have you been?"

Harold explained to Jack that because the KGB had bugged the room, and unexpected visitors, like the cleaning lady, were common, the hotel cell wasn't a place he wished to spend his time. When Harold and Jack returned to their room, Harold pointed to the wires peeking through the plaster and to a decorative flower hiding a tiny microphone. Harold placed a water glass over the flower and banged on it with a spoon.

Jack laughed and imagined the reverberations thumping on hidden ears. He leaned over the flower, "Hey Harold," he said, "help me with this new secret code machine!"

"OK, Yerman," replied Harold, "but wait, I can't put this fuse together. Could you hand me that wire?"

Harold was on a personal mission to aggravate the Russians. The same pointy-nosed KGB agent tailed the pair each time Jack and Harold left the hotel. Jack and Harold named their new friend "The Weasel." The agent followed the Americans everywhere. One day, Harold dragged Jack to the Kremlin. Harold opened doors, entered offices, and collected a crowd of anxious bureaucrats who followed the Americans through the corridors until they grew tired and ushered the athletes out. The Russians were direct and clear. No visa would be forthcoming.

One hundred thousand spectators filled the stadium on the first day of the two-day competition. The highlight of the meet, the most published event of the competition, was the duel between UCLA's student body president, Rafer Johnson, and Russia's decathlon star, Vasily Kuznetsov. Rafer was the most celebrated athlete on the American team. When he was a teenager in California, he had attended a track meet and had watched the event featuring running, throwing, and jumping; he thought to himself, *What's the big deal with this? I could win this thing* (Dancier). He had been winning ever since. After two days and ten grueling events, Rafer emerged the victor, shattering his own world record and beating Kuznetsov's unofficial record (UPI, 1958). The Soviets in Lenin Stadium stood and cheered the two decathletes who embraced. The ice of the Cold War briefly softened.

Telegram: "DON'T LOOK AT ANY BACKS
AND RUN LIKE HELL LUCK AND LOVE. MARGO—"

The closing event featured the 1,600-meter relay. Jack ran the first leg in 46.7—fourteen meters in front of his competitor, followed by Tom Courtney, Eddie Southern, and Glenn Davis. The Americans defeated the Russians by forty-five meters on a muddy track with a time of 3.07.0 (Bloom, 1958). The American men won the meet with a score of 126 to 109. The American women took four of ten events against the chemically enhanced Russians, but the U.S. ladies lost 44 to 63.

The final score appeared on the electronic scoreboard: USSR 172, USA 170. The Americans were dumbfounded! The Russians had agreed to mark the competition as two dual meets, one between the men's teams and the other between the women's; but when the Russians combined the scores, they changed the rules and the U.S. lost (Musel, 1958). Communism declared a great victory over democracy; the next day papers around the world would tout the Soviet win. Jack, like most of the other U.S. athletes, felt cheated.

Jack and Harold headed back to their room, banged their fists on the flower a few times, and made grumpy remarks about Russians into the microphone. The athletes felt better knowing that a spy on the other end was recording their frustration.

Someone knocked at the door. "Jack, are you expecting anyone?" asked Harold.

"No, you?" responded Jack.

Harold moved to the door, turned the knob, and pulled it open. The Weasel, escorted by another Russian, whom the American team knew as John Roman, stood smiling with a bottle of vodka in hand. John Roman was the lead agent assigned to watch the Americans.

Harold looked at the men, then down at the jug. "Come on in," he said.

Drinking is a sporting event in Russia, and two large Russian weight men carrying more vodka sauntered into the room behind John and The Weasel. They started drinking and talking to Harold. As the liquor flowed, tongues loosened, and John Roman shared that he had learned his perfect English when he was eleven years old from downed WWII American pilots he hid from the Germans, fed, and eventually helped escape.

Jack watched Harold raise his jug and match the big men drink for drink. The group talked about World War II, the Iron Curtain, Khrushchev, Eisenhower, the Cold War, and sports.

The conversation turned to Olga and what she might do if she ever made it to Czechoslovakia.

"She's just visiting family," explained Harold.

At five a.m. the Russian weight men lay unconscious on the floor, and Harold was still going strong. The Americans grabbed their bags and said goodbye to John Roman and The Weasel. They left the hotel for the airport bus and on to Poland. The team left the city limits as the sun burst onto a new day.

The lingering acrimony from the meet's results had not yet faded. The group exchanged few words as it watched the landscape shift past the windows, when, without warning, the bus pulled to the side of the road and stopped. A green sedan rested at a diagonal in front of the bus with its hood towards the shoulder of the road. Jack watched the bus driver's white knuckles release their grip from the steering wheel and pull the door lever to allow The Weasel to climb aboard. The agent's bloodshot eyes systematically scoured the group until he found Harold sitting in the back. Without saying a word, he walked to the back and handed Harold a parcel. The Weasel turned and exited the bus. Harold opened the envelope, pulled out papers, and looked through them. He grinned and stood up, "Olga's going to Czechoslovakia!" The bus broke into cheers.

Indeed, Olga and Harold had received visas, but they were "transit visas," allowing them to stay in Czechoslovakia to visit her parents only a few hours in the airport until the next plane departed (Connolly, 2012). It would be fifty years before Olga returned home for a real visit. Harold and Olga worked every conceivable angle to recognize her native citizenship, but they could not break the Cold War prejudices. Olga received a letter from the Czech Olympic Committee stating that it no longer considered her a citizen because she could not train in Prague. Olga recalled, "Then, I realized that I'd been told 'no.' I was crushed, mainly because I'd promised something to the president and had no way to explain it" (Willoughby, 2008).

Olga became a U.S. citizen, and eventually her parents were allowed to join her in America. Olga competed for the United States' Olympic teams in the Rome, Tokyo, Mexico City, and Munich Olympic Games. In Rome, her former teammates shunned her. She would not understand "why" until eight years later, in Mexico City:

I learned [in Rome] that somehow everybody was angry with me, because the Czech athletes turned away and wouldn't talk to me.... Then, much later, in Mexico City, I met a group of Czech athletes. I looked at them, they looked at me, and so I said hello to them in Czech. They all knew me, or had heard about me, and they started talking to me, and then one said, "All right, how was it? Did you really fly the coop, or did they give us a pack of lies about you?" I told them that I hadn't run away and told them what had happened. It was only then that people began to understand that it had only been claimed that I had refused to compete, when, in fact, I was not allowed to compete (Willoughby, 2008).

Olga's proudest moment as an athlete came at the 1972 Olympic Games in Munich when she carried the American flag at the opening ceremony. She said, "I believe in a democracy that the flag belongs to everybody, so I felt like I was representing every person in the United States" (The golden girl, 2006).

Fifty years after earning her country an Olympic gold medal and a world record in the discus, the Czech Olympic Committee reunited her with teammates in her homeland. Olga said of the occasion, "My emotions are high. I'm overwhelmed to tears. I think it's extremely gracious, and I'm happy." She added, "I believe in the Olympic Games. I believe in the Olympic ideal. I believe that the Olympics will survive spiritually. I think I've given a lot of my life to promoting the Olympic philosophy of brotherhood and sisterhood of humanity" (The golden girl, 2006).

CHAPTER 7

The Rendezvous

[A young man] must have good stuff inside to keep his wits about him. He is called upon at eighteen to make decisions which would challenge those much older and wiser. It is to the everlasting credit of our athletic youth that so many of them turn out well in spite of so many temptations put in their way.

Coach Brutus Hamilton
(Walton, 1992)

The flight to Warsaw, Poland, was short. The team arrived at its hotel before noon. Four hundred friendly Polish fans asking for autographs surrounded the Americans. Twenty-two thousand would watch the dual meet over a two-day period, and Jack would run against the fastest 400 sprinter in Europe that night. He was tired from last night's negotiations and needed rest. He pushed through the mob, received his room assignment, and slept.

Wham, wham, wham...
Jack was startled awake by a rapid knocking on his door, *What now...?* he wondered.
Jack staggered to his feet and cracked open the door to find Dee Givens, the Oklahoma State sprinter, greeting him with an ear-to-ear smile. Dee, who had been injured in practice and would not run, had decided to occupy his time sightseeing.
"Yerm, you're my bud, aren't you?" demanded Dee in his distinctive southern drawl.
"Yeah," Jack said wiping the sleep from his eyes.

"Then get your stuff on. I need your help. I've got us a *rendezvous* with two girls, and they won't budge unless I get a friend, and *you* are my friend."

"I'm tired, Dee, and I have to run tonight," Jack replied.

"Well, just come and take a look. That's all I ask," said Dee.

Jack groaned, invited Dee to wait for him, and put on his street clothes. Dee led Jack out of the hotel to a small corner cafe. Two petite, cute, full-bodied girls with bouncy poodle haircuts sat waiting in a booth. One was a redhead with green eyes and the other a blue-eyed blonde. Jack wasn't tired anymore.

"Jack, I'll take the redhead; you can have the blond," announced Dee.

The attractive girls offered to show the boys the city. They helped the Americans exchange money on the black market. Jack's pockets bulged like a hamster's cheeks that had just found the mother lode. He hired a taxi for a dollar a day and bought a steak lunch for twenty-five cents. The girls took the Americans to the remnants of a Jewish World War II ghetto and to a workshop that made expensive Polish glass.

Jack and Dee decided to show the rest of the team what a couple of real operators could accomplish in a short period of time. They gave the girls tickets to the track meet and made plans to take them to the black-tie dinner honoring the Polish and American teams after the meet. The Americans performed well. Jack won the open 400 and ran a fast 46.2 in the second leg of the 4x400.

After the meet, a taxi dropped off the two couples at the hotel. The "men" strutted down the hallway to the grand ballroom with their dates clinging to their arms. The doorman welcomed Jack and Dee, announced their arrival, and placed their invitations on the silver tray. All eyes focused on the girls, but Jack was not prepared for the glares that followed. Conversations halted; it was as if the tinkling of champagne glasses stopped and the orchestra faded. An angry Polish official rushed over and ordered, "Get those girls out of here. Now!" The girls cried, strong Polish words were exchanged, and the boys pulled the girls back to the street and hailed a taxi.

Jack could not make sense of what had happened, nor did he understand what the girls and the official had said to each other. The sobbing girls would not disclose anything. Jack felt at odds; instead of showing up at the party like a couple of operators, he and Dee had embarrassed their dates. They decided to rescue the evening and take the girls to a nightclub.

The nightclub was in the basement of a stone-grey gothic castle dating back to the fifteenth century. The girls excused themselves to the powder room, leaving Dee and Jack to discuss the evening. A stranger approached the table and introduced himself as a British national working for Reuters News Agency. With a touch of antipathy, he queried, "What do you know about those girls?"

"Well, they *are* pretty," Dee responded with his broad southern smile—his eyebrows lifting.

"Yes, they are very beautiful, but do you know *anything* about them?" asked the man.

"No, we don't really know anything," interceded Jack before Dee could boast again.

The man pulled out his business card and wrote a phone number on the back. He gave it to Jack with instructions, "I want you to call this number at the American Embassy and ask for Major Brock. He's the Marine Security Officer and will have some information for you." The man turned and was gone.

The boys walked over to the black phone box hanging on the wall. Jack inserted a coin, turned the dial marking the numbers, and the phone rang: "American Embassy, Sergeant Smyth speaking." After talking to a second sergeant, he waited until Major Brock came to the line. "Who are you and what is the problem?" His demanding voice sounded far away.

"We're with the American track team and on a date with two attractive Polish girls," explained Jack.

"Describe the girls," barked the major over the scratchy connection.

Jack described the blond and the redhead in detail.

"Do not wait to hang up," insisted the major. "Move! Get out of there! Do not talk to those girls. You are the targets of two female Polish secret-police agents. *They want something!*"

"Thank you, sir," responded Jack in his best ROTC voice. Jack hung up, turned to Dee and looked directly to his eyes. "We run!" he said.

"No," Dee argued. "No way. We stay. I'm from Oklahoma, and I know how to handle this."

Jack never understood what sort of special knowledge boys from Oklahoma had in dealing with Polish secret agents.

"Jack, listen to me," Dee retorted, unfolding his arms to free his hands for exclamation. "You see, we know who the girls are, and the girls don't know that *we* know who *they* are! Let's tease them for a while. It'll be fun."

The girls walked back to the table. Their makeup was back together and their confidence restored. Jack and Dee quickly learned what their dates wanted. They would be vindicated if the boys would take them to the next party at the American Embassy. Jack surmised that the girls had hoped to become familiar faces at the ball and would be invited to other U.S. parties later. They wanted access to people, specifically embassy diplomats.

At Dee's persistence, the boys decided to see the girls again the next day. The girls continued to apply pressure for an invitation to the party. Later, Jack told his date what Major Brock had reported and that he believed she was with the Polish secret police. She protested, "No, I am not!"

The boys said their goodbyes and would not see the girls again.

Two years later, Jack sat reading a magazine at Bancroft Library on the Berkeley campus. A recent spy case had made national news. It confirmed Major Brock's warning to the boys.

On December 5, 1959, it was Irvin Scarbeck's turn to work the night desk at the American Embassy in Warsaw. He was alone, the phone rang, and he picked it up. A young woman's voice greeted him—a rich, whispery Polish accent speaking English. He had been warned to beware of phone calls from strange women. "It is a favorite approach used by lady spies," they had told him in his orientation. The young woman on the phone asked something about a visa, and he decided it would be best to deliver the information personally. He made arrangements to meet her on a nearby street corner.

He found the girl—her blond hair cut in the popular bobbed style of the day. Her large eyes were soft and inviting. She laughed easily, and she stood close to the middle-aged diplomat. Her rose perfume captivated his senses and heightened his awareness of her tight sweater and short skirt that left little to Irvin's imagination. His devotion to his German wife and their three children faded in her mesmerizing presence. He asked her name.

"I'm Urszula Discher," she said. She was twenty years old and explained that she lived in the back of a store, not far from where they stood.

He made arrangements to rendezvous again. He eventually rented a private apartment for her on Koszykowa Street in Central Warsaw, two blocks from the American Embassy, and they began a fourteen-month romance (AP, 1961).

On the evening of December 22, 1960, Communist agents broke into the apartment and photographed Scarbeck and the girl together in bed. The Polish police threatened to jail her on charges of being an unregistered prostitute. Irvin Scarbeck was the second secretary at the embassy. He was responsible for much of the daily operations as well as having access to classified information. Two Polish officers, who were known to him as Zbigniew and George, threatened to jail Miss Discher and expose the American if he did not provide classified information to save his unfortunate lover. He succumbed to their demands.

Irvin explained to Urszula that the work of spies was a chess game, and he would find a way to get her out of Poland. He arranged for a friend in West Germany to send a telegram to Urszula claiming her non-existent brother lay dying in a Frankfurt hospital. Scarbeck negotiated with the Polish authorities and traded more secrets to obtain a visa for the girl. Urszula flew ahead of her man but went straight to a Frankfurt boarding house used by Communist agents as a secret rendezvous (Parade, 1962).

Scarbeck was reassigned to Italy and was unaware that American counterspies had placed microphones in his office and had collected the needed information to arrest him. He was summoned to Washington for meetings. FBI agents descended upon him as he walked the capitol's streets. Urszula was extradited to the Unites States to testify at the trial. Scarbeck claimed that he had betrayed his country only to help the young woman escape Poland. He refused to believe that she was involved with the secret police. The whole of the United States was riveted on the titillating scandal, and every small-town newspaper printed a photograph of the fair Urszula Discher and carried news of Irvin Scarbeck's conviction and thirty year sentence to prison—the first American Foreign Service officer ever caught in a treasonable act. Shortly after the trial, the young girl, who previously had wanted out of Poland, quietly returned to Warsaw.

Decades later, Rink Babka spoke to Jack at the 2011 Mount Sac Relays banquet in Pomona. The U.S. 1960 Olympic track team was honored for breaking five world records and six American records at the tune-up meet before leaving for Rome. As the men sat reminiscing, Rink asked Jack, "How did two guys like you find such cute girls in Warsaw on that trip?" Babka had been the team ladies' man, handsome, and the best dressed, and he still wondered, half a century later, how Jack and Dee had found the blond and the redhead. Jack shared the story with Rink and mused, "I wonder, what ever happened to the redhead?"

CHAPTER 8

Would the World be Different?

You can blame the [Berkeley] student strike for this long screed. I am presently in the Dean's office but the building is closed and all appointments have been cancelled while the staff tries to clean up the mess following yesterday's sad and bewildering events. The building is a mess.

You may have forgotten that you were once given the assignment (in addition to your other duties) to see that a certain Special Assistant to the Dean of Students should not become a bitter and disillusioned old man. You may have to get busy soon for the person in question reaches the mandatory retirement age in July of '65 and he's complaining. Says he's no longer able to keep his finger on the pulse beat of student thought and attitudes, doesn't understand their poetry, their art, their philosophy, their demands or their attitude of mind. He's not bitter yet but may be just a little disillusioned. Since there's not much time perhaps you had best begin to make plans to straighten him out and bring him up to date. He hasn't quite reached the point of that sad old Japanese poet-statesman of the 16th Century who wrote the Haiku poem,

> *"Between the washing bowls of birth and death*
> *How many words I've spoken; what a waste of breath"*

But he may be on his way to that stage.

Coach Brutus Hamilton
(Hamilton, 1975)

In the spring of 1959, Jack's junior year at Berkeley, he had extra time on his hands. Jack had decided not to play football in order to prepare for the Olympic Trials, and without the routine of practices, scrimmages, or team meetings, he needed something to do—

something that would make money. When Jack learned that the student body president earned a respectable $3,000 a year, he decided to run for political office. Where the student council met was a mystery to him, but he needed a job, and he believed that no one truly cared who was president. "Hey, I can win this one," he told Margo. Although she had doubts, she signed on as his campaign manager.

Margo worked with the Associated Students as Director of Student Publicity and Public Relations. She knew something about student government; so, with her help, Jack set off to conquer the ASUC presidency. They began by meeting with an ex-president, Roger Samuelson, and developed a platform that proposed more married-student housing and invited renowned speakers to the University.

The candidates grew to three. There was Dan Lubbock, a member of several clubs, John Schaefer, a pre-law and business student, and Jack, with "No affiliations with any radical, fraternal, or conservative political group," wrote a reporter in the campus newspaper (Slate Program, 1958).

Jack and Margo followed the traditional Berkeley campaign pattern: "Take the candidate to the students." Margo took Jack to the sound of clinking silverware and glasses, the aroma of baked potatoes and gravy, and an occasional, "Please pass the salt." Jack and Margo visited students in dorms, fraternity houses, and sororities who paid little attention while they ate dinner. It mattered little because there was nothing remarkable in this race—until Dave Armor showed up.

Dave represented everything that Jack and the other candidates did not. He was a political science major and part of SLATE,[*] a new campus political party that entered the contest with a candidate for every post and a liberal affirmative action and equal rights platform (Slate Program, 1958). The source of SLATE's funding was a mystery, but it had a printing press, rented office space, and mobilized professors and students. The SLATE machine joined the race with deep pockets and challenged the traditional candidates who had few resources and a university-imposed thirty-dollar spending limit (Editor, 1958).

---

[*] SLATE is capitalized in documents remembering the movement, although the papers at the time wrote it as "Slate." Both versions are found in this chapter depending on the source. SLATE is not an acronym, but rather refers to the "slate of candidates."

Armor pressed the ASUC to take a stand on off-campus issues (Cal Students Rights Qustioned, 1959). Jack retorted, "All aspects of student welfare—our interests in city, state, and national issues—should not be pursued by the Student Association." Armor asserted that the sports program should be recreational and managed by the student government (Slate Program, 1958). Jack countered, "It would be foolish to put a multi-million-dollar athletic program that brings prestige to the University and its students into the hands of novices. Organized intercollegiate sports build character, provide support and entertainment for students, and generate revenue for academic programs. Intercollegiate sports are the showpiece for wider fundraising and scholastic efforts. The program must have a dedicated, dependable, and professional administration."

SLATE candidates spoke out against the establishment and traditions. The University was synonymous with insensitive government; SLATE's defiant rhetoric against the *status quo* establishment moved Student Association President Bill Strickland to request that the University withdraw official recognition from SLATE:

> The University of California must be a place where laws are changed by lawful means, not defied by mob action. It is the responsibility of this university to guarantee that the students who pass through its halls do not leave with a warped view of how lawful society operates. Lawful society demands remedies for the open defiance of laws and regulations.
>
> I request that University of California official recognition be withdrawn from the group of students known as Slate. I further request that University of California official censure be imposed on these individual students who carried out the defiance rally of Thursday, March 12, 1959(Stricklin, 1959).

E.E. Stone, Dean of Students, ruled that student groups were not to take positions regarding off-campus issues. San Francisco Assemblyman John A. O'Connell requested an informal opinion regarding Stone's ruling from the State of California Attorney General's office. The attorney general ruled that SLATE could not be prohibited from engaging in off-campus political activities, although the University may prohibit the use of its facilities. Furthermore, the American Civil Liberties Union became interested in the controversy (Off-Campus Political Activity Considered Legal for Slate, 1959). Powerful groups now had a stake in SLATE's success.

An obscure conflict in Southeast Asia, in tiny Vietnam, had found its way into the newspapers. SLATE argued against sending America's youth across the sea to fight someone else's battles. The Bay Area press began covering the Berkeley campus elections. Meanwhile, SLATE continued to grow, using the off-campus office to coordinate commuter students. The candidates debated in the school's traditional free speech area, on the question, "Should Cal student government be involved in off-campus politics?"

The excitement grew daily, and a new issue surfaced that brought national attention to the race. SLATE challenged Berkeley students to denounce, and even withdraw from, the National Student Association, which was "a front for the Central Intelligence Agency." "Mr. Armor has gone too far on this one," said Jack to Margo. "We'll get him!" Jack defended the National Student Association as an upstanding organization representing students' interests in Washington.

Armor raised the rhetoric, "The National Student Association is a tool of the CIA!"

Jack believed he had the election—until disaster hit. At a press conference on the East Coast, a few days before the election, a reporter asked Allen Dulles, Director of the CIA, a question: "There's an election going on in Berkeley where one of the candidates says the National Student Association is linked to CIA. Is that so?" Dulles answered the reporter by acknowledging that the CIA gave the Association money each year for students to study in Iron Curtain countries, and, in exchange, the CIA received reports on the economy, morale, and structures within those countries. This statement hit Jack—and the rest of Berkeley—like a boulder. All eyes were on the election, and it grew to be the biggest election in the school's history. Jack realized he was out of his comfort zone. He began to fear the responsibility of the office if he actually won.

Tuesday, May 12, a record 5,622 students went to the polls. Armor received 1,769 votes and Lubbock pulled a close 1,517 to qualify for the runoff. The other two candidates received too few to continue: John Schaefer earned 1,150 votes, and 587 students voted for Jack. (Armor, Lubbock in Presidential Finals, 1959). The next day Coach Hamilton, with a grin and a twinkle in his eye, said, "Jack, not many men can claim 587 friends."

Voters found Dave Armor more compelling and voting for SLATE more exciting. Armor won the final election by a slim thirty-three votes (Armor Wins—Closest Vote Ever, 1959), and SLATE took over student politics at Berkeley. Students were ready for a liberal take over; after all, the youth of America supplied the army with its warriors. Many were not willing to put their lives on the line for a war they did not understand.

Looking back, Jack had seen signs that the campus was changing. Berkeley sat on federal land, and as such, required that young men enroll in ROTC. Jack, having grown up in a neighborhood that honored returning World War II heroes, had never doubted his responsibility to participate in ROTC. The government also gave him a uniform that included sturdy black shoes that he needed for school and an extra dollar a day for serving as an upper classman cadet officer in command of a thousand men.

Each month, on a Thursday, thousands of students, dressed in their uniforms, paraded in front of the reviewing stands. Jack's shoulders were square, and his breast swelled with pride as his men marched in step across the baseball field and made the big turn in perfect order towards the observation deck lined with colonels and generals. On a brisk spring Thursday, Jack's battalion marched as they had done many times before, with heads turned sharply to salute the Sixth Army. To the shock of those in the reviewing stand, and to Jack, the men dropped an assortment of women's panties and bras in front of the reviewing area, strewn the length and breadth of the company. Within a year of the election, SLATE challenged compulsory ROTC enrollment (Slate Raps Latest Issues, 1959); their timing was perfect.

SLATE toured campuses across the state to propagate its politics to students at UCLA, Riverside, and Santa Barbara.

It organized defiant political groups in the face of conservative opposition:

> The [SLATE] meeting reached a climax
> when the UCLA student body president
> accused Slate of "fomenting strikes
> and riots."
>
> Slate arrived at Riverside Saturday to
> find that a warning of their visit had
> preceded them. Stamped across the top
> of the student activities bulletin
> distributed to all students were the
> words "Beware of Slate"….
>
> [Santa Barbara] Student body president
> Kitty Joyce said at an executive
> committee meeting last week "the
> Associated Students did not invite
> them and did not want them." A faculty
> member defined Slate for the council
> and said it was "a political-action
> group of students with outside
> support, which appears to have as its
> intent the obstruction of virtually
> every official position taken by the
> University administration."
>
> He went on to say, "Slate is
> interested in destroying the
> University as we know it. We are old
> enough to get our own show," he
> said(Slate Finds Support, Suspicion On
> Tour, 1959).

Back in Berkeley, unusual people drifted into the city, camping along the sidewalks of Telegraph Avenue. They would later be known as flower children. The youth of America questioned blind patriotism. They challenged the United State's role in world affairs, while others declared, "We won't take anything from those long-haired freaks." The world's eyes remained focused on what Berkeley would do next—and it soon had its first Free Speech riot; then came the drugs, the anti-establishment movement, the civil rights and anti-war movements, protests and demonstrations, and the youth of America crying, "Make love not war!" Berkeley was at the heart of "groovy." There were "love-ins," "sit-ins," "happenings," and "hippies."

Jack watched the social unrest move across the United States and wondered whether there might be a shrouded scheme to start trouble in America's universities. Certainly, if the CIA could send students to foreign schools through the National Student Association and gather information, why wouldn't other governments do the same—maybe even upset the American establishment?

Several years later, Governor Ronald Reagan used his handling of the unrest in Berkeley to prove his law-and-order stance and to gain national prestige. In April of 1969, an eclectic group of young people "reclaimed" a parking lot owned by the University of California. The group tore up the asphalt, planted a garden and several trees, set up a swing set, and built benches. People's Park was born. Reagan ordered them off the land, and when they refused, he sent in the National Guard.

One of the protestors was shot, and the incident exploded into an insurrection of six thousand people. The National Guard evacuated, and the park remains today as an icon to the counter culture where the flower children, although much grayer and slower today, linger in the psychedelic sunshine of their victory. The University of California's halls whisper echoes of those early activists.

In retrospect, it all began with SLATE—and Jack, having been at the crossroads of the Free Speech Movement, muses, "If I had won, would the world be different today?"

CHAPTER 9

Olympic Trials and Tribulations

It's easy to be intense in competition.
It's difficult in practice these cold, rainy and lonesome days.
But project yourself forward—these are the days that count.
These are the days when champions are made.

Coach Brutus Hamilton
(Hamilton, 1975)

Jack trained through the fall and was feeling good when tragedy struck. His campus job required moving equipment at gymnastics meets. After a meet with UCLA, Dave Epstein, another 440 runner, and Jack pushed the bulky vault across the gym floor. They lifted the apparatus onto a piano dolly, maneuvered it across the floor, and then aimed for the doorway. The dolly jammed on the doorframe, and Dave pushed harder with a grunt and a shove. The vault skidded off the dolly and landed with a thud on Jack's big toe. "Ouch!" The pain shot up his leg, and he reacted instinctively, lifting the vault off his damaged foot in one swooping reflex. Jack's face grimaced; he pivoted on his good foot, his bad foot averting the floor (Herman, 1960).

Jack turned and limped down the hallway to the office of Jack Williamson, the athletic trainer, who gently removed Jack's black and white Chuck Taylor and pulled off his sock. The blood had collected under the opaque toenail, and, as his foot felt the cool air, the throbbing pain crawled up his leg.

"We've got to relieve some pressure," said Williamson as he drilled a tiny hole into the nail and a lucid mixture of red fluid oozed relief from Jack's damaged foot. Jack sat on the table, put his shoe on, and limped ten blocks uphill to his fraternity, but his tender toe continued to swell. He asked a friend to drive him to the Student Health Services at the nearby Cowell Hospital where he remained for several days. He lost his toenail, a serious problem for a runner. *The San Francisco Chronicle* published a photo with Jack gazing at his foot. The caption read, "GET WELL BIG TOE."

His condition grew worse when his well-tuned muscles favored the injury, throwing off his muscular symmetry, creating new aches and pains throughout his body. Jack's world-class training program halted to a remorseful stop. Jack watched his teammates for the next two weeks prepare for the regular season while he stretched and jogged slowly until the swelling and tenderness disappeared and his big toe had healed. Jack began the track season racing against Keith Thomasson, a Stanford athlete who had run a 46.2. Jack had not practiced since the accident. He ran and lost.

Jack trained with renewed vigor. The smell of the track, the crisp spring air, and the spectators wearing hats and sunglasses with programs in hand were all a welcome return to normalcy. He felt strong, just in time for the Pacific Coast Conference meets. Jack's pent up energies peaked at the Modesto Relays. "I'm ready," Jack whispered as he knelt in the blocks. The cracking sound of the starter's gun reset his senses, like one of Pavlov's animals, and Jack shot out like a thoroughbred. His team of four broke the world record in the sprint medley relay.

The Olympic Trials would be held across the Bay at Stanford University. An athlete who finished in the top three of his event would then qualify for the Olympic team. Jack had three opportunities to qualify for the Trials: (1) he could place in the top seven in the NCAA championship meet; (2) he could place in the top five at the national open trials; or (3) he could qualify by placing in the top three at the military trials.

Jack decided to run the 400 meters at the NCAA meet held in Berkeley where he had home advantage, and a week later he would travel to the AAU National Championships in Corpus Christi to compete in the 800. If he should qualify for both, he would decide which to run at the Olympic Trials at Stanford, because running both in the 1960 Olympics was not an option.

Head Coach
Brutus Hamilton

The NCAA heats at Berkeley were scheduled for Thursday and Friday, and the finals on Saturday. Jack felt strong and in shape in spite of starting late in the season. His times were among the fastest in the nation. Coach Hamilton sat in the stands for a pre-event meeting on Monday with every college coach that had a runner in the NCAA finals. Jack approached Brutus and asked, "What's the workout for today, Coach?"

"Warm up. Then we'll try a few hundreds."

Jack reported to the end of the track and jogged toward the starting line with his hand raised in the air as a signal to Coach Hamilton that he was ready; he accelerated to the line and dropped his hand. Brutus, watching from the stands, clicked his stopwatch, and again clicked when Jack sprinted across the finish line in front of the coaches, "9.7." Jack felt terrific and jogged back for another run. He approached the start again, dropped his hand as the aggregate of coaches clicked their watches. He crossed the finish line and heard the collective buzz, "9.6!" When he ran the next time, a hundred watches clicked in unison, and a combined "Ooh!" rose from the bleachers. Jack ran a 9.8. Three impressive times back to back and he felt great! Jack continued to run hundred-yard intervals, and the watches kept clicking—Jack's adrenaline, endorphins, muscles, and mind melded together, and consumed in the aura of a runner's high, he whispered to himself, "I can do this forever!"

Jack crossed the finish line the sixteenth time in 9.8 seconds. "Jack, that's enough. It's time to go in," said Coach Hamilton.

"Go?" Jack questioned. "I'm not tired, Coach."

"We'll call it a day, Jack," said Hamilton. "You're ready for Thursday."

During the night, Jack's muscles protested and tightened. The fibers in his legs were not ready for the physical intensity his mental resolve had demanded. Morning greeted him with his legs as stiff as fence posts. He sat up and willed his feet to the floor. His calves, his quadriceps, his hamstrings, and his glutes screamed back at him. He could hardly stand. Jack panicked, "How stupid! What am I going to do?" He asked a roommate for a ride to the locker rooms. There, Jack Williamson massaged his muscles, sat Jack in the whirlpool, packed his legs with analgesics, and stretched Jack's muscles. But nothing would reverse the damage. Jack's confidence crashed—again. Neither Jack nor Coach Hamilton realized that getting caught up in running in front of the country's coaches would have such serious consequences; they had showcased Jack's ability, but in so doing had exceeded his physical capacity.

Jack felt heavy and tired for Thursday's heats. Only the top four of eight runners would advance to the next round. Jack ran 47.8 and finished fourth. Jack slowed to a 48.2 on Friday but still managed a fourth place finish.

On Saturday, the day of the finals, his legs would not bend. Walking was painful. His muscles screamed in protest. Jack skipped the warm up. Seven of the final eight athletes would advance to the Olympic Trials in two weeks, and he knew that it would take a miracle to beat just one runner—one of the best in the country. Jack knelt down in the starting blocks and wished he could disappear. He had no strength remaining in his legs. When the starter's gun fired, Jack staggered to the vertical position only to watch the field of athletes move away. He had worked for a chance at the Olympics, the pinnacle of an athlete's career. His dream faded with the disappearing runners. He must, at least, finish the race, pushing as he did years ago when, as a boy, he ran across a freshly plowed field simply to see whether he could do it. He was racing alone, against his throbbing muscles.

Jack was ten meters behind the other runners at the 200 mark and out of contention—but at that moment, a runner grabbed his leg and fell to the track. *What's happening?* thought Jack. The athlete's face grimaced. *Had he pulled a muscle?*

Jack limped past the injured athlete and miraculously qualified for the Olympic Trials (Wilson, 1960).

Few people had known the extent of Jack's injury (Bergman, 1960). Reporters, coaches, and athletes only guessed at how he might run in the trials. Jack remained secluded in Berkeley for the next two weeks, staying at Hamilton's house rather than crossing the Bay Bridge to Palo Alto and training with the other athletes. Brutus cared for the entire wellbeing of his boys; he watched out for them on and off the track. He was like a father—a disciplinarian and a counselor. Coach Hamilton was careful with his athletes, but Jack's debilitating stiffness surprised them both. Brutus's program had already worked miracles in Jack's short season. There was no better place for Jack to become whole again than under the care of Brutus and his wife, Rowena. Brutus had a way of working his athletes to peak at the right time. Jack was fundamentally strong, was in shape, and needed to synchronize his mind and his muscles. A week before the meet Coach Hamilton believed Jack was ready to run harder. They quietly set the schedule to peak the day of the Olympic Trials.

The Trials at Stanford drew the largest crowd ever to see a track meet in the United States since the 1932 Olympic Games in Los Angeles. Sixty-five thousand filled the stadium for the finals with a two-day total of 106,000 (Wilson, 1960). Jack won his heat in 46 flat. The final race would be run in less than an hour. The fanatical track nuts argued over who would win. Would it be Otis Davis or Teddy Woods (Wong, 1960)? No one considered Jack a contender, but his training had prepared him for the day's tight schedule.

Other athletes stretched, jogged, paced back and forth, and tried to stay warm between the races. Jack found a shady spot under a training table. He felt the refreshing breeze touch his forehead. He rested until the call came for the eight fastest quarter-milers in the country to report to the track.

Each of the eight runners had an individual story of long training hours, obstacles, and a dream of running in the Olympics. Each stood waiting in apparent coolness, but inside nerves twitched and minds focused. "Runners, to your marks," called the starter in the white cap. The athletes moved up to the starting blocks. Some shook their arms, others looked to the heavens, and all set their feet in the blocks. The eight runners knelt in position as if praying to a higher source. Jack looked up and focused on the white lines framing his lane. The man lifted the starter's gun. "Set!" he bellowed, and the runners lifted their backs to the sky. The man paused for a moment and then squeezed the trigger.

The eight runners blasted out of the blocks. Arms pulsated and legs flew around the first curve. As quickly as the sweat beaded on the athletes, it evaporated in the speed as they sprinted around the track. Jack was in fifth place at the 200-meter mark. The Bay Area track fans had seen Jack come from behind in other races. Knowing spectators pointed and predicted, "Now watch this Yerman. You will think he's part of the pack, and then toward the end, he'll pour it on."

They were not disappointed. He surged, his muscles held together, and he burst out with forty meters to go. The track nuts shouted, "I told you so! I told you so!" "Come on, Yerman! Come on!" "Show 'em what you've got!" "There he goes! There he goes!"

Jack edged Earl Young by two-tenths of a second to win in 46.3 (Wong, 1960). Enthusiasts recorded Yerman as having run the two fastest consecutive 400 meters, the trials and the finals, on the same day (Bloom, 1988).

The upset victory brought Margo running from the stands and onto the infield where she hugged Jack and gave him a congratulatory kiss in front of sixty-five thousand spectators. Margo looked at the reporter and simply said, "I am so happy!" She already had her tickets to Rome and would leave the following week (Durslag, 1960).

The Sacramento Bee sports writer captured the moment:

```
Big Surprise. Jack Yerman of Woodland,
University of California senior, not
only qualified for the Olympic Games
team, he upset the dope all over this
huge stadium to win the 400-meter run.
```

Yerman gave up a promising football career to concentrate on track. He barely qualified for these final trials two weeks ago when he finished far back in the National Collegiate Athletic Association championships.

"I felt tired that day," said Yerman. "Today I had it."

Asked how he trained for yesterday's race, Jack smiled and said: "I guess I didn't train at all. I just took it easy so I would have it when it counted. This was the race of my life" (Adams, 1960).

Jack (219) edges out Earl Young
Olympic Trials

The 1960 U.S. Olympic track team was the strongest and the strangest group of athletes. Wacky pole-vaulter Don Bragg hoped to be Hollywood's next Tarzan. The charismatic athlete had cleared fifteen feet nine and a quarter inches for a new world record and celebrated by thumping his chest like a bull ape. This brought "Jane" racing out of the stands into the ample arms of her beloved jungle fiancé. They both danced before Don signed hundreds of autographs: "*Tarzan Bragg*" (UPI, 1960).

Tom Murphy made the Olympic team by winning the 800-meter run and throwing up as he always did; Lieutenant George Young, the winner of the 3,000-meter steeplechase, where athletes jump over barriers and almost clear the water hazard on the other side, would be going to Rome. George had never seen the event until a year earlier when he surmised that this was something he could do. George had practiced for hours jumping over bales of hay at his ranch in New Mexico until he had mastered the art of the steeplechase.

Bill Nieder was a big disappointment at the meet. The mountainous man had gone back and forth with Olympian Parry O'Brien over the past year for world records in the shot put. Bill held the current record at sixty-five feet seven inches. The U.S. coaches had planned on stacking the team with Nieder and O'Brien, but Nieder injured his leg and failed to qualify. The coaches awarded Bill the precarious status of "alternate." This was a meaningless position because no alternate had ever been promoted. The U.S. Olympic Committee wanted Bill in the Games, and when Dave Davis, the athlete who made the team, injured his hand while lifting weights, the Olympic fathers unloaded Davis in favor of Nieder. The move confirmed a clear message to the rest of the team: "If you are injured, sick, or falter, do not let it be known." Jack had injured his knee in the 400 victory. If the coaches found out, he might be replaced. Jack trained for three days, the pain intensified, and he rested for two.

The Olympic team held practice meets in Eugene, L.A., the Bay Area, and shattered a number of world records; at their last meet in Walnut, California, Jack anchored the mile relay against another set of Olympians. He came from behind to beat Glenn Davis, the world-record holder in the 400-meter hurdles. Jack's foursome set a new world record in 3:05.2.*

It was time for Europe. The United States Olympic Committee loaded the U.S. track team onto a fleet of sluggish prop planes. In contrast, the U.S. officials travelled in luxurious jets. "Sending the

---

* In April 2011, members of the 1960 U.S. track team returned to the Mt. SAC meet in Walnut, near Pomona, as Guests of Honor in remembrance of the Fiftieth Anniversary of the 1960 performance.

team on the props saves money," they said, "and we need to arrive early to make arrangements."

In the near future, the U.S. officials' arrogant attitude would grow into a series of errors that would cripple the greatest track team ever assembled.

CHAPTER 10

The Olympics in Rome

When ideals are obscured in amateur sports, then comes the danger of an athletic injury to the character of the athlete.

Coach Brutus Hamilton
(Walton, 1992)

When Jack was nine years old, and every summer until he turned fourteen, he signed up for the YMCA summer camp. A youth counselor, Don Bloom, befriended the small boy. As a teenager, Jack played basketball and ping pong at the Y Center in town where Don worked. Don became the sports writer for the *Woodland Daily Democrat* and eventually reported for *The Sacramento Bee* in the state's capital. Don, who had promoted Jack in the press, took it upon himself to raise funds to send Jack's mother to the Olympics in Rome.

Local Drive at $728. Every day it becomes more evident that Woodland is a pretty doggone nice place to live.

Community spirit our little city does not lack. Yesterday another local club and 14 individuals added $116 to "Send Mrs. Yerman to the Olympics" drive. These donations pushed the fund total up to $728 and really opened the door to achieving the goal of $1,300.

The   drive   is   now   .562   percent
complete. It is picking up at an even
faster tempo than earlier in the week.
Daily totals have gone from $317 to
$438 to $511 to $612 to $728.

If   you   aren't   one   of   the   54
individuals or a member of one of the
five   clubs   who   have   joined   the
campaign, you are more than welcome to
send   your   donation   to   "Democrat
Olympic   Tour   c/o   Mrs.   Yerman."
I guarantee you'll sleep easier when
you realize you've added to a most
worthwhile local drive(Bloom, 1960).

The list of contributors grew and the money poured in. The
woman who worked nights, who never owned a car, who had never
taken a vacation, joined a group of eighteen from Woodland and
travelled to Rome to see Jack compete (Bloom, 1988).

Irene kept a meticulous journal throughout the trip. She
noted particulars that would seem mundane to experienced
travelers, but for her, the small details were an adventure. She kept
a list of what she ate, the color of the blankets in the hotel, the
shape of the bathtub faucets, the temperature of the water, the
oxygen panels above the seats in the airplane, and what time the
sun set:

*August 29th, 1960. Luggage wgt. 34 lbs. Entered plane directly from
airport. Pretty stewardesses. Canteens for workers at airport. 8:45 on our
way. No room under seats for flight bags. 9:30 a.m. over Nevada; 10 a.m.
coffee, coffee cake; 10:15 a.m. Salt Lake. River? Nebraska? Platte River?
12 noon Lunch—Tomato, sea food salad-peas, brown stew—peach with
crumbs, graham cracker? Whipped cream—coffee; corn with rice....*

Jack travelled with the American track team from New York to
Switzerland on a chartered prop plane. The rested officials had
arrived earlier in modern jets and greeted the weary-eyed athletes
who unfolded themselves from their cramped conditions. The
officials whisked the Olympians to a warm-up meet that afternoon.

The team rested only a short night before boarding a train for a fourteen-hour journey to Rome and the historic Olympic Games.

The Olympics were born in ancient Greece, 776 BC, from a single footrace near the banks of the Alpheus River at Olympia. The priests presented the champion, Coroebus, with a wreath of wild olive leaves woven from the twigs of a tree that Hercules had planted in the sacred grove near the Temple of Zeus. The Olympics Games were a religious event, honoring the gods through perfection—the perfect body of an athlete in sport. The Greeks hailed their Olympic heroes as idols in life and revered them as gods in death. All competitors had to declare that they were freeborn Greeks without taint or suspicion of sacrilege against their gods (Kieran & Daley, 1961).

Boxing, wrestling, chariot racing, and the marathon were added over the centuries to the original 200-meter footrace. An Olympic stadium was built that held nearly fifty thousand spectators. Men competed without clothing. Women were not allowed to attend the Games until the mother of Pisidorus, a winning athlete, was discovered in the stadium watching her son. Pisidorus's mother had become his trainer when her husband died. She attended her son's race in disguise but could not contain herself when he won. Death was the penalty for such a crime, with victims thrown off a nearby cliff. In this case, the judges deemed the mother's cause honorable and spared her life. Women eventually participated in the Games, and Belisiche, a woman from Macedonia, won the chariot race in the 128th Olympic Games.

Scandal crept into the growing games. Theagenes, a priest of Hercules and all-around boxing champion, was disqualified when he cheated during a match. Upon his eventual death, the townspeople honored their local hero with a statue. One night, a jealous rival, who had never defeated the great Theagenes, pushed the bronze likeness over. It wobbled in the wrong direction and fell, crushing the angry man. Another boxer killed his opponent in a final bout through a deliberate trick. The judges disgraced the athlete and gave the victor's crown to the dead man. Boxing scandals continued in the 98th Olympic Games. Eupolus of Thessaly bribed three opponents to let him win. He was discovered, disgraced, and fined. But the greatest punishment for him and others who violated the Olympic code was to be immortalized in statues called *Zanes* (Kieran & Daley, 1961).

Their frozen images were carved in marble and placed at the entrance of the Olympic stadium with captions warning all athletes to remain true and faithful to the religious and competitive spirit associated with the Games. Our word *zany* is derived from these dishonorable symbols.

The Games lost their religious significance over time as athletes sought gifts and money rather than the sacred olive wreath and respect from the gods. Greece faded before the grandeur of Rome, and the Olympics lost their importance. The Romans held competitions from time to time until Emperor Theodosius I terminated the games by decree in 394. Barbarian invaders would pillage the Olympic temples. A century later earthquakes completed the destruction, changing the course of the Alpheus River to rise and bury the hallowed plain where the first event had been run.

The 1960 Olympics returned to Rome after a 1,500 year absence. Rome had a millennium to prepare for the resurrection, and there would never be a venue so beautiful. The marathon ended in the shadows of the ancient Coliseum under the Arch of Constantine. The gymnastics competition took place in the ruins of the Baths of Caracalla, and wrestling was staged amid the visages of the once imposing Basilica of Maxentius. This was a beautiful city where centuries joined to contribute to the backdrop of the largest and most celebrated Games to date. Jack Yerman, a young man from a small town in California, stood in Rome to witness the convergence of history, architecture, and sports.

The Italians constructed *Villaggio Olimpico* for a record 7,725 athletes from 87 nations (UPI, 1960). It was a city within a city, complete with shopping centers, parks, play areas, landscaping, and a network of roads. The track and field events would be held in the modern Olympic Stadium that seated one hundred thousand spectators.

At a time when the United States was trying to make sense out of Jim Crow laws that sent Negros to the back of the bus and to separate drinking fountains, Rafer Johnson, Jack's teammate, all the more notable because he was black, carried the Stars and Stripes leading the red, white, and blue American team into the stadium. Each country traditionally dipped its flag as a tribute to the host nation when the delegation of athletes marched past the Tribune of

Honor. Rafer did not dip his flag, and since the American colors did not dip, neither would the Russians lower their flag. The Soviet team marched into the stadium led by a square-jawed heavyweight who stiffly held the flagpole at arm's length (Kieran & Daley, 1961). The tensions between the two superpowers gave way to the Olympic spirit when the flamboyant Italians entered to an enthusiastic crowd. The Olympics had returned to Rome!

The Italians' flair for beauty and enthusiasm were evident everywhere to everyone. A reporter wrote of their fervent spirit at the twenty-kilometer racewalk finish line:

> **ROME, Sept. 4 (UPI)** Briton Stan Vickers swears the next time he finishes the 20-kilometer competitive walk he'll remain upright, no matter how exhausted he is.
>
> After placing third in the Olympics, he laid down to rest. He was immediately seized by non-English-speaking ambulance men and rushed to a hospital on the outskirts of Rome.
>
> It took British officials several hours to find and "rescue" him (UPI, 1960).

These Games were the first to be televised around the world; new heroes emerged in the homes of every-day Americans. People in New York, Ohio, Wyoming, and California watched Wilma Rudolph sprint to gold. Wilma had suffered double pneumonia and scarlet fever as a child. She was number seventeen of nineteen children. She had been sickly and weak and wore a leg brace until she was eight years old. She discovered basketball, and her strength, coordination, and talents blossomed. Wilma set a high school state record scoring forty-nine points in one game (Roberts). She would go on to win three gold medals for the United States, running a fast 11.0 seconds in the 100-meter sprint and 24.0 in the 200-meter sprint. She anchored the 4x100-meter relay for an easy world record (Kieran & Daley, 1961).

The most historic event in the modern Olympics is the men's marathon, dating back to 490 BC. That was the year the Greek General Miltiades led nine thousand Athenians and a thousand allies to meet an even greater army of Persians near the city of Marathon. The Greeks fought for their wives, their children, and their country and pushed the fleeing Persians back to the sea. The elders gathered in the Athens market during the battle to await the news of whether their city would be safe or destroyed. Miltiades summoned a messenger, Pheidippides, to carry the news of victory. Pheidippides had fought through the torridity of battle. He tossed his shield aside, stripped himself of his armor, and sprinted for Athens. Inspired by the good news, and in spite of weary muscles, parched lips, and overwhelming fatigue, he raced the 26.2 miles, arriving exhausted and staggering into the city. At the feet of the elders, and deathly short of breath, he delivered his message: "Rejoice; we conquer!" Pheidippides fell to the ground, gasped for air, and died (Kieran & Daley, 1961).

Years later, when Jack recounted his experience of the 1960 Games, he shared the story of the marathon runner who became a legend for his outstanding performance and his abilities to overcome adversity. The five foot nine inch, 128-pound Ethiopian shepherd, Abebe Bikila, who turned down an offer of shoes, ran barefoot over Rome's pavement and cobblestone streets through the night while Italian soldiers held torches to light the way. Bikila won in a record time of two hours, fifteen minutes, and seventeen seconds and became Africa's first black Olympic medalist and a national hero in his homeland. Emperor Haile Salassie promoted Bikila to the rank of captain of the Ethiopian Imperial Guard.

Bikila ran the 1964 marathon in Tokyo, but this time he wore shoes, and, in spite of an emergency appendectomy a month before, he surpassed his previous record by more than three minutes. He finished the race by performing jumping jacks to show the crowd that he could have run further (New York Times, 2000). In the 1968 Mexico City Olympics, Bikila would leave the marathon after seventeen kilometers. His coach reported that Bikila had suffered a bone fracture in his left leg several weeks before and had not wanted it known (Guide to Black History).

Bikila's life unexpectedly changed in 1969. Critically injured in an auto accident and after months in the hospital and numerous spinal operations, he resigned himself to a wheelchair. Bikila said of his accident, "Men of success meet with tragedy. It was the will of God that I won the Olympics, and it was the will of God that I met with my accident. I accepted those victories as I accept this tragedy. I have to accept both circumstances as facts of life and live happily" (Dibaba, 2007). Bikila took up archery and competed in the Paraplegic Games. He died in 1973 at the age of forty-one from a brain hemorrhage. News of his death shocked the world, but his legacy lives as Africans continue to compete and win in his shadow.

Expectations for the "greatest American track team ever assembled" were high, but the team performed poorly in the Olympic heats; and in contrast to the hoopla before the trip, the Americans received a whiplash of negative press. Headlines read:

American Trackmen "Choked-Up" Say Russians

ROME, Sept 4 (AP)..."The Greatest danger for any sportsman is to be afraid," Litovev (coach of the Soviet hurdlers) said in an exclusive interview tonight.

The Americans came here expecting to defeat everyone. When they found they could not do it, they became afraid(AP, 1960).

The world could only guess why the Americans fell short. Percy Cerutty, Australia's eccentric distance coach, speculated, "I don't think the Americans expected this heat. It has hurt the Australians as well" (AP, 1960).

The record breaking temperatures and high humidity played a role in the track team's demise, but it was not nearly so significant as the anxiety the American officials imposed upon the team. The prop plane, the quick warm-up meet, the long train ride, and bad water sapped the Americans of their strength and gave way to dysentery. Jack, like so many others, had trouble keeping liquids in his system. He was sick, but he did not dare share his condition with those who could administer medication. He and the others were afraid that they would lose their places on the team if they showed weakness as Dave Davis had after the Stanford trials. Jack's California teammate and close friend, Jerry Siebert, ran the 800-meter semi finals with a 101 degree fever and diarrhea. He was eliminated. The press vilified sprinter Ray Norton (AP, 1960), who ran out of his zone during the 4 x 400 finals, but he, like many on the team, was far from top form. Meanwhile, newspapers back home reported that the Americans were disloyal to their country, passing the time with "wine, women, and song" (Tonelli, 1958). Coach Hamilton, sitting in Berkeley, read the reports and later quipped, "I knew all along that the claims were untrue. Jack and Jerry can't sing worth a lick."

Journalists tried various methods of entering the Olympic Village to speak with the team. One male sportswriter, dressed up like a female athlete, was discovered and tossed out (Bloom, 1988). Don knew he needed to speak with Jack and attempted to enter the front gates, but the guards, with hands on guns, stared him down, so he found another way. Outside, Don ran into "Mutt and Jeff" of the USC track team—little Max Truex at 5 feet 5 inches and 128 pounds and the American record holder in the 10,000 meters, and gigantic Rink Babka at 6 feet 5 inches, 267 pounds, who had won silver in the discus. Don told them how badly he needed to get into the Olympic Village.

"Don't worry about the security," Babka told Bloom, "Put on these ID pins. Athletes wear them to get in and out of the gate" (Bloom, 1988). Don pinned the pass on his lapel and gave his wife the other pin. He lifted his chin, stood tall, and pulled the shoulders of his slight build back. His wife said he looked like a fencer, and she pretended to be a gymnast. They walked through the gates with a group of athletes, and inside they nearly stepped on Jack before recognizing him. Jack's cheeks had sunk, his complexion yellowed, and he walked head down, running into Don. He was very sick.

"It's great to see someone from home—" Jack's voice cracked.

"What's the matter with you? You're so thin."

"I've lost fifteen pounds. I felt strong in Pomona, but the trip has been hard." Jack told Don the team was drained of strength, and his knee was swollen. "I'm afraid if they find out," said Jack, "they won't let me run. We're all sick from the food and water. The Russians were smart," continued Jack. "They brought their own water, and none of them is sick" (Bloom, 1988). Jack's spirits lifted after talking to someone from home.

Jack won his first two heats in 47.2 and 46.4, but the illness prevailed and he finished last in the semi-finals at 48.9, a second slower than he had run three years earlier as a high school senior. It took all of Jack's strength to finish the race far behind the others. The 400 was over for him. He dragged his dehydrated body back to the Village—to escape the people, the hot weather, and his disappointment in sleep.

Ticket to Olympic Stadium

Don's Woodland group had traveled six thousand miles to see Jack win a gold medal. Jack had one more chance: the 1,600-meter relay, the final event of the Olympics. Would the American officials replace him? Years later, in his book *Confessions of a Sportswriter*, Bloom recalled the race:

No, because Coach Larry Snyder knew Jack's reputation for being more outstanding as a relay runner than when he was running for himself only. He was named to run the first leg in the race in which either the U.S. or Germany would have to break the world record to win. With him were 400-meter champion Otis Davis, sixth-placer Young and Glenn Davis, who had won his second Olympic 400-meter hurdles title. Germany boasted 400-meter silver medalist Carl Kauffman, fifth-placer Manfred Kinder and two more excellent one-lappers in Hans Reske and Johannes Kaiser.

When Jack got into his starting blocks, I felt more nervous than he appeared. Looking through binoculars at the man I counseled when he was a youngster at YMCA camp before becoming an internationally known athlete, I could see he was far from being in peak physical shape. I had known him since he was a shy boy growing up in a broken home, was dedicated to his mother and determined to better himself in scholastics and athletics. In his eyes I saw that burning desire that made him the only man to compete in the Rose Bowl, Olympic Games and Pan American Games. He deserved a gold medal. I said a quick, silent prayer.

At the gun, Yerman sprinted into the first turn like a man possessed by the devil. He had the spark. Running against Reske, he sped around the track as if it were the last race of his life. When an obviously exhausted Yerman handed the baton to Young, Uncle Sam's team was seven yards ahead of fourth-place Germany. Yerman's time was 46.2, the fastest opening lap in Olympic history. America went on to win a world record in 3:02.2 to Germany's 3:02.7. In my mind, that half-second margin was because of Yerman, but of course, I was slightly prejudiced.

Mrs. Yerman was even more proud as she stood tall when the giant scoreboard flashed the names of the American team; the foursome walked to the top of the victory stand and the national anthem was played in their honor. With Margo Brown, who would become his wife, also in the stands, Yerman wore a wide smile as Old Glory was raised. He came—and he conquered. It was a race and a day I'll never forget.

I often wondered what it would be like to stand at the top of the victory stand. Several years later Yerman explained, "There are some similar highs. It's a combination of what you feel with the birth of your first son, college graduation, getting married and coming home after years of absence. When the flag is raised and the anthem is played, there is a bond that exists between the crowd and the athletes. This bond is as if everyone, for a brief moment, is a member of the nation of mankind" (Bloom, 1988).

Irene sat in the stands wearing her new sunglasses and taking in the sights and sounds of the victory. She recorded the day and the event in her journal:

Sept. 8, 1960: Afternoon meet—cloudy. Hotel Michelangelo—luxury! English speaking people. Visited fruit and vegetable market—shops. Javelin throw—women's high jump. 1600 Meter Relay: threatening rain. Put on rain gear—hoping it wouldn't pour, at least until race over—no one left—sprinkling. Gold medal, whole stadium on their feet.

World Record Olympic 4x400 Team, left to right –
Earl Young, Otis Davis, Glenn Davis, and Jack Yerman

In the glow of the win and with gleaming gold medals around their necks, the four champions walked out of the stadium to a small warm-up field. The men stood together and received congratulations from coaches, trainers, and fellow athletes. An Italian photographer, one of the infamous *paparazzi*, moved in and asked handsome Earl Young, the youngest of the four, to hold something. Earl instinctively received the object, when, without warning, little Coach Eastman leapt forward and hit Earl like a linebacker. The object flew from Earl's hands and crashed to the ground, releasing the acerbic smell of strong alcohol. There, at his feet, lay a shattered bottle of whiskey. Jack realized that if the staged photo had been taken, it would have appeared in newspapers around the world where many were willing to believe that frivolous parties were the reason for the team's poor performance. The Americans were only a camera flash away from a scandalous photo and a cunning caption that might have read: *Earl Young, USA Olympic Gold Medal Winner, Celebrates.*

The Games ended with the United States' thirty-four gold medals to Russia's forty-three. The president of the United States Olympic Committee, Avery Brundage, charged the athletes with "getting too soft and complacent," and the cry of "wine, women, and song" was shouted again (UPI, 1960). When Jack looked around the Olympic venue, he imagined a statue of the duplicitous American officials immortalized, like the Zane statues of old, for dishonoring the Olympic spirit.

CHAPTER 11

The Victory Lap

The book is closed, but not quite. Indulge me some more. Across our sinful, grasping lives has come the sweet breath of fresh air for which I hoped and prayed.... No one of the thousands who saw or the millions who heard the Games but what was cleansed and ennobled in spirit because of it. Who knows, my dears? Who knows? Maybe the prophet Isaiah who said, "How fair upon the mountain are the feet of them that bring glad tidings."

Coach Brutus Hamilton
(Hamilton, 1975)

When Jack told his roommate, Jim Ring, that he would be taking Margo to Woodland on the Greyhound bus to a parade in his honor, Jim replied, "Yerman, you gotta go in style. You're driving my new Corvette!" Jack did not argue.

The clear California autumn morning had begun to warm. Jack drove with the convertible top down, pushed his foot on the accelerator, and felt the horsepower surge within the little red Corvette. Margo's dark hair fluttered as they drove east on Interstate 80 from the Bay Area towards the city of Davis. The betrothed couple had dated for three years without owning a car and was happy for the rare occasion of riding alone. Margo's engagement ring sparkled from her hand; she would not wear it publically until the engagement party to be held in their honor that evening in Woodland.

All of Woodland had followed Jack to the Olympics. Now, children ran a little faster, the high school football team practiced a little harder, and the Leithold Drug Store seemed a little busier. Mayor Frank Heard proclaimed this day, the twenty-first of October, as Jack Yerman Day:

WHEREAS, Jack Yerman has given outstanding service in sporting activities to Woodland High School and the City of Woodland;

WHEREAS, Jack Yerman has made similar accomplishments as a member of the University of California Track Team; and

WHEREAS, Jack Yerman did win a position on the United States Olympic Team; and

WHEREAS, Jack Yerman brought great acclaim to himself, his country, his school, and his home town as a member of the winning 1600 meter relay team in the Summer Olympics at Rome, 1960; and

WHEREAS, The City of Woodland is extremely proud of its Olympic Gold Medal winner and wishes to pay all tributes possible;

NOW THEREFORE BE IT RESOLVED that the City Council of Woodland, California, does hereby proclaim Friday, October 21, 1960, as "Jack Yerman Day" through the City of Woodland and does urge all Woodland citizens to join in the salute to Jack Yerman.

PASSED AND APPROVED by the Woodland City Council this 17th day of October, 1960.

Frank E. Heard
Mayor, City of Woodland

Posted in Woodland

Jack turned off I-80 onto 99 North to Woodland. The car glided over the two-lane highway that separated fragrant peach orchards and earthy sugar beet fields. Mesmerized by the warming day and cadenced patterns of the agricultural rows, Margo's mind wandered back to the remarkable events of that summer:

Jack handed Margo a fistful of wadded bills before she left for Europe. "I've been to Europe before," he said, "and I know you can always use extra money. Take a ride to the top of the mountain, or do something special." They had talked of marriage, and Margo understood the request.

Margo travelled with Babs Feiling, her close friend and former college roommate. When the girls toured Amsterdam, the diamond capital of the world, it seemed a natural place to look for a ring. Margo window-shopped jewelry stores until she spied a petite .18 karat gold, single band, with a .21 carat offset diamond. The thought of the ring brought her back to the window several times. She tried it on. The gold band curled around her finger, and rather than forming a perfect loop, one end gently lay over the other, like a gold ribbon resting on her finger with a small, solitary diamond sparkling from the top. I'd rather have this than a ride to the top of a mountain, she thought. Later, Margo left Babs in an art museum and secretly bought the ring for $125 dollars.

The girls timed their trip to arrive in Rome a week before the Olympics. Margo and Babs caught the attention of the Italian men; shopkeepers reached up and pinched their youthful faces, and men on public transportation could not keep their claws off the two beauties, leaving the young ladies fuming from the pinches and bruised bottoms. The guards at the Olympic Village, possibly concerned with making a good impression, assumed the girls, with their bobbed hair, were American swimmers and allowed them to enter. Margo visited Jack and his teammates, and when no one was looking, she handed a non-descript package containing the wedding ring to Jerry Siebert, who quietly passed it on to Jack.

Jack welcomed time with Margo. They cheered for the Greco Roman wrestlers in the ancient redbrick Baths of Caracalla. They attended an opera with live horses and a Roman chariot. They explored Rome's streets and found their way to the Trevi Fountain where Neptune entered the city on a magnificent seashell pulled by massive horses; and like thousands before, they turned their backs to the water and tossed coins over their shoulders. Legend has it that by so doing, they would someday return to Rome.

Margo and Babs occasionally ate with American friends in the cafeteria designated for American, Canadian, and British athletes, until an Italian official wised up to the ruse, and, flanked by two security guards, made a beeline for the girls. He shook his finger at the imposters and, in broken English, demanded that the girls leave. Margo and Babs gathered their things and walked to the gate. (Later, when the rumors of "wine, women, and song" surfaced, Margo believed the Italian official assumed she and Babs were prostitutes.)

Immediately following the Olympic Games, the men's track team flew to Athens to compete in an exhibition meet. Margo, who had minored in Latin in Berkeley and was well versed in both Roman and Greek mythology, welcomed the offer to join the team in Athens if she could get herself there. The night after the 4x400 victory, Margo headed to Greece, where she would meet Jack, and booked a closet-sized room in the basement of the same hotel where the American team would stay.

Jack arrived with the team in Athens the next day, and the young couple ate dinner at a small rooftop restaurant. The warm night carried their conversation while a violin played in the corner. They ordered dolma, the traditional small bundle of spicy meat and rice wrapped in sweet grape leaves. After dinner, they strolled to the Temple of Zeus with its majestic columns. Jack pulled the ring from his pocket and turned to Margo. He held her hands and asked, "Will you marry me?"

Her eyes sparkled, and she said, "Yes!" They kissed. The next day they purchased a watercolor of the ruins of the Temple of Zeus from a street artist as a keepsake.

Turning the Corvette onto Woodland's Main Street brought Margo back to the moment. Margo removed her ring and slipped it into her purse. The champion had arrived in his chariot with his damsel by his side. Just as at the end of an Olympic race, when the athlete jogs around the track in victory, it was Woodland's turn to celebrate.

Jack returned to his home a Collegiate and AAU All American, the United States 400-meter champion, and a world-record holder. This was the most spectacular athletic career ever accomplished by a Woodland High School graduate. Jack was the only athlete in U.S. history to compete in the Olympic Games, the Pan American Games, and the Rose Bowl, and the only trackman in the world to run on teams that set world records in the mile, two-mile and 1,600-meter relay events. Moreover, he ran with the University of California team that clocked the fastest ever sprint medley relay and was one of a few athletes to compete against the Soviets in the USSR (Bloom, 1960).

Jack gratefully acknowledged his home town at the luncheon hosted by the Woodland Chamber of Commerce:

> Woodland has a fine tradition of friendship, and I'll always be grateful. The highest honor I've ever received came from the people of Woodland. This came to me when you sent my mother to Rome to see me compete in the Olympic Games. This was the high point in both our lives, and we'll forever be grateful. I wish I could personally thank everyone who has helped us.

Jack paused for a moment and looked down the guest table to his mother. The handkerchiefs came out in every corner of the room when he said:

> I especially want to thank my mother—for being my mother. You've always stood by me from the beginning and especially on the bad days (Bloom, 1960).

There would be more speeches, and half of the city's population lined the streets to wave to Jack, who led 103 entries in the largest homecoming parade to date. Jack's classmate and friend, Pat Welty, in charge of the Class of '56 float, stood proudly on the decorated truck bed, wearing Jack's dark blue Olympic sweats and holding an Olympic torch. After the parade, Woodland High held a pep rally and the homecoming football game.

Bill and Bethel Griffith invited guests to their home for a celebratory dinner before the night's big game. Visitors arrived to a sign Bethel had posted on the front door that read, "Jack and Margo, A Winning Team!" Inside, flickers of light bounced from Margo's engagement ring, surpassed only by her radiant smile. Jack's mother, Irene, sat off to one side of the room, still in wonderment at the far off places she had seen and the thrill of her son's successes. Jack's sister, Kathy, ebullient as ever, laughed and talked easily with friends. Margo's sister, Karen, who had driven from her desert home in Taft to represent Margo's parents, chatted with fellow Taftian, Jan Smith, a Cal song leader and Margo's dear friend. Well wishers included

Don Bloom, the sports writer and years earlier young Jack's YMCA counselor, and Bob Griffith, Bill's brother, who just a few years ago had interviewed the eager boy at the drug store, and Coach Brutus Hamilton, who taught Jack life's lessons on the track and would continue his friendship for many years. Guests embraced the Olympian and his smart, spunky, and beautiful fiancé.

Jack's time had come.

Jack and Margo
A Winning Team!

Works Cited

Adams, W. (1960, July 3). "Yerman is Upset Victor in 400." *Sacramento Bee*, p. D 1.

AP. (1958, July 19). "U.S. Trackmen Leave for Russia Tomorrow." *Bakersfield Californian*, p. 18.

AP. (1958, July 2). "Yerman Wins for U.S. in Swiss Meet." *Oakland Tribune*, p. 45.

AP. (1960, September 5). "American Trackmen 'Choked-up' Say Russians." *Los Angeles Times*, pp. IV 1-2.

AP. (1960, September 23). "Ray Lost Weight, Too." *Bakersfield Californian*, p. 11.

AP. (1961, October 5). "Spy Trial Hears of Blackmail of Envoy." *Oakland Tribune*, p. E 3.

"Armor Wins—Closest Vote Ever." (1959, May 18). *The Daily Californian, 170*(68), p. 1.

"Armor, Lubbock in Presidential Finals." (1959, May 13). *The Daily Californian, 170*, p. 1.

"Athletes Americains a Lausanne." (1958, Juin 27). *Feuille D'avis de Lausanne*, p. 27.

Bergman, R. (1960, June 22). "Slight Summer Guide to Bay Area Athletics." *The Daily Californian*, p. Sports Section.

Bloom, D. (1958, August 2). "Yerman Hands To Courtney & Hail the Conquerors." *Woodland Daily Democrat, Sports News*.

Bloom, D. (1960, October 22). "325 Cheer Yerman at CC Luncheon." *Woodland Democrat*, p. 1.

Bloom, D. (1960, August 20). "Don Bloom's Scoreboard." *Woodland Daily Democrat*, p. 9.

Bloom, D. (1960, October 21). "Olympic Champion Yerman Feted During Homecoming." *Woodland Democrat*, p. 1.

Bloom, D. (1988). *Confessions of a Sportswriter*. New York: Vantage Press, Inc.

"Cal Students Rights Qustioned." (1959, March 17). *The Daily Californian, 170*(30), p. 1.

Chong, L. (2006, October 6). *The Sunday Times*. Retrieved August 7, 2011, from The Times: http://business.timesonline.co.uk/tol/business/industry_sectors/banking_and_finance/article663342.ece

Dancier, T. (n.d.). *I Can Do Better Than That!* Retrieved August 7, 2011, from Colored Reflections: http://www.coloredreflections.com/decades/Decade.cfm?Dec=1&Typ=2&Sty=1&PID=724

Dessena, G. M. (1958, luglio 8). "Un 800-record mancaato ed Altre cose ruiscite." *La Gazzetta dello Sort*, pp. 1-2.

Dibaba, A. T. (2007, August 8). *Afro Articles*. Retrieved August 8, 2011, from afroarticles.com: http://www.afroarticles.com/article-dashboard/Article/Abebe-Bikila-s-Identity-Theft-and-Amharas-Refuted-by-Oromo-Intellectual-Asafa-Dibaba/38633

Duguid, S. (2012, June 9). *Olga Fikotova, Czechoslovakia*. Retrieved October 14, 2012, from FT Magazine: http://www.ft.com/cms/s/2/a194b7a2-adfc-11e1-bb8e-00144feabdc0.html#axzz29E1XEUN3

Dumas, A. (2010). *The Count of Monte Cristo* (Nook E-book ed.). Barnes & Noble.

Durslag, M. (1960, July 3). "From First Sports Page." *San Francisco Examiner*.

Editor. (1958, April 11). "Slate Strikes Again." *The Daily Californian*, p. 8.

Grinczel, S. (2003). *Michigan State Football, They are Spartans*. Charleston, South Carolina: Arcardia Publishing.

Guide to Black History. (n.d.). Retrieved August 8, 2011, from Encyclopedia Britannica: http://www.britannica.com/blackhistory/article-9002541

Hamilton, B. (1975). Dear Freinds and Gentle Hearts; London, August 5, 1952. In L. J. Black, *The Worlds of Brutus Hamilton* (p. 76). Los Altos, California: Tafnews Press.

Hamilton, B. (1975). From Remarks Delivered at Marin Sports Injury Confernece; March 10, 1962. In L. J. Baack, *The Worlds of Brutus Hamilton* (p. 58). Los Altos, California: Tafnews Press.

Hamilton, B. (1975). Instructions to Shotputers. In L. J. Baack, *The Worlds of Brutus Hamilton* (p. 44). Los Altos, California: Tafnews Press.

Hamilton, B. (1975). Letter to Avery Brundage, November 28, 1953. In L. J. Baack, *The Worlds of Brutus Hamilton* (p. 81). Los Altos, California: Tafnews Press.

Hamilton, B. (1975). To Jack Yerman. In L. J. Baack, *The Worlds of Brutus Hailton* (pp. 23-24). Los Altos: Tafnews Press.

Hamilton, B. (1975). To Kathy Buchanan; December 4, 1964. In L. J. Baack, *The Worlds of Brutus Hamilton* (p. 120). Palo Alto: Tafnews Press.

Hamilton, B. (1975). To Lee Covington. In L. J. Baack, *The Worlds of Brutus Hamilton* (p. 29). Los Altos: Tafnews Press.

HammerThrow.org. (n.d.). *Harold Connelly*. Retrieved October 12, 2012, from http://hammerthrow.org/about-us/harold-connolly/

Herman, S. (1960, March 30). "Hamilton is not Disappointed Despite Losses and Hurts." *The Daily Californian*, p. Sports Section.

IISRP. (n.d.). *Elastomers Shaping the Future of Mankind*. Retrieved August 7, 2011, from International Institute of Synthetic Rubber Producers, Inc.: http://www.iisrp.com/WebPolymers/00Rubber_Intro.pdf

Ives, D. (1958, September 19). "Crippled Bears Fire-Up for First Test." *The Daily Californian*, p. 4.

Kieran, J., & Daley, A. (1961). *The Story of the Olympic Games, 776 B.C. to 1960 A.D.* Philadelphia: J.B. Lippincott.

Lenin, N. (1905, December 3). *Socialism and Religion*. Retrieved July 3, 2012, from Marxist Internet Archive: http://www.marxists.org/archive/lenin/works/1905/dec/03.htm

Litsky, F. (2010, August 10). *Harold Connolly, Who Beat Odds in Olympics and Romance, Dies at 79*. Retrieved from The New York Times: http://www.nytimes.com/2010/08/20/sports/20connolly.html

Marannis, D. (2008). *Rome 1960: The Olympics that Changed the World*. New York: Simon & Schuster.

Martin, D. P. (1958, juin 28). "Meeting USA." *Programme Officiel*. Lausanne.

Maxwell, N. (1968, March 26). "Teeter Totter Twins May Tackle World's Record." *The Daily Californian*, p. 2.

Musel, R. (1958, July 29). "Moscow Results Leave Everybody Happy." *The Bakersfield Californian*, p. 25.

New York Times. (2000, October 1). "Ethiopia Establishes Tradition in Men´s Marathons." Retrieved August 8, 2011, from *New York Times*: http://www.nytimes.com/2000/10/01/olympics/02MARATHON.html

Oakland Tribune. (1958, October 12). Photo.

"Off-Campus Political Activity Considered Legal for Slate." (1959, April 8). *The Daily Californian, 170*(30), p. 1.

"Parade." (1962, January 7). *Oakland Tribune*, p. 12.

(1979). Proverbs 22:1. In *Holy Bible* (King James Version ed.). Salt Lake City: Intellectual Reserve, Inc.

(1979). Proverbs 25:17. In *Holy Bible* (King James Version ed.). Salt Lake City: Intellectual Reserve, Inc.

Roberts, M. (n.d.). *Rudolph Ran and the World Went Wild*. Retrieved August 8, 2011, from ESPN.com: http://espn.go.com/sportscentury/features/00016444.html

"Slate Finds Support, Suspicion On Tour." (1959, November 17). *The Daily Californian, 171*(46), p. 1.

"Slate Program." (1958, March 3). *The Daily Californian, 166*(20), p. 1.

"Slate Raps Latest Issues." (1959, December 3). *The Daily Californian, 171*(56), p. 8.

Stricklin, B. (1959, March 17). "Stricklin Requests Chancellor Action." *The Daily Californian, 170*(30), p. 1.

The Daily Californian. (1958, October).

The Daily Democrat. (n.d.). *Obituary.* Retrieved February 6, 2012, from The Daily Democrat, Woodland, CA.: http://www.legacy.com/obituaries/dailydemocrat/obituary.asp x?n=robert-leithold-griffith-bob&pid=148281779

The golden girl. (2006, December 20). Retrieved October 15, 2012 from http://www.praguepost.com/archivescontent/2813-thegolden-girl.html

Tonelli, C. (1958, September 23). "Seibert, Yerman: View on the Olympics." *The Daily Californian.*

U.S. Census Bureau. (n.d.). *Historical Census of Housing Tables; Home Values.* Retrieved February 4, 2012, from Census of Housing: http://www.census.gov/hhes/www/housing/census/historic/values.html

UPI. (1958, July 29). "Moscow Joins Kingsburg in Acclaiming Johnson". *Bakersfield Californian*, p. 25.

UPI. (1960, August 14). "87 Nations to Compete." *Los Angeles Examiner*, p. 1.

UPI. (1960, September 5). "Ambulance Crew Eager For Work." *Los Angeles Times*, p. V 2.

UPI. (1960, September 12). Games Failures Spark 'Crash Program'. *The Bakersfield Califronian*, p. 31.

UPI. (1960, July 23). "U.S. Fields Strongest, Zaniest Olympic Team." *Progress-Bulletin*, p. 1.

Walton, G. M. (1992). *Beyond Winning; The Timeless Wisdom of Great Philosopher Coaches.* Champaign, Illinois: Leisure Press.

Willoughby, I. (2008, January 5). *Olga Fikotova-Connolly: 1956 Olympic champion dubbed "traitor" in communist Czechoslovakia over romance with US athlete.* Retrieved October 14, 2012, from Radio Praha: http://www.radio.cz/en/section/special/olga-fikotova-connolly-1956-olympic-champion-dubbed-traitor-in-communist-czechoslovakia-over-romance-with-us-athlete

Wilson, D. (1960, June 19). "Ten NCAA Marks." *San Francisco Chronicle*, p. 29.

Wilson, D. (1960, July 3). "Yerman's 46.3 Wins 400-Meter." *San Francisco Chronicle - Sporting Green*, p. 17.

Wong, B. (1960, July 1). "Greatest Show On Earth Unfolds." *The Daily Californian*, p. 4.

Wong, B. (1960, July 8). "What 106,000 Fans Will Never Forget." *The Daily Californian*, p. 4.

Yerman, J. (1958, July). Letter To Margo Brown. Lausanne.